Annie Crossfoot.

KU-005-172

MANAGING DIRECT MARKETING

MANAGING DIRECT MARKETING

Philip Mounsey and Merlin Stone

Croner Publications Ltd
Croner House
London Road
Kingston upon Thames
Surrey KT2 6SR
Tel: 081–547 3333

Copyright © 1990 P Mounsey and M Stone
First published 1990

Published by
Croner Publications Ltd.
Croner House,
London Road,
Kingston upon Thames,
Surrey KT2 6SR
Telephone: 081–547 3333

All rights reserved.
No part of this publication may be reproduced,
stored in a retrieval system, or transmitted in any form or by
any means, electronic, mechanical, photocopying, recording
or otherwise, without the prior permission of
Croner Publications Ltd.

While every care has been taken
in the writing and editing of this book,
readers should be aware that only Acts of Parliament
and Statutory Instruments have the force of law,
and that only the courts can authoritatively
interpret the law.

British Library Cataloguing in Publication Data
Mounsey, Philip
Managing direct marketing.
1. Direct marketing
I. Title   II. Stone, Merlin, *1948*–
658.81

ISBN 1–85452–077–6

Typeset by Input Typesetting, Wimbledon
Printed in Great Britain by
Whitstable Litho Ltd., Whitstable, Kent

Contents

Foreword

This book is a significant step forward in the achievement of quality in marketing. In British Telecom, we insist on the highest standards in the management of our communications with customers. To achieve this, we combine all media and project manage our campaigns so that customers get the right communication at the right time, with the right message. The processes to achieve this must be clearly specified. This book shows how to use management processes to achieve high levels of quality in direct marketing — combining traditional direct marketing media with the most rapidly growing medium — telemarketing. I wish the reader all success in implementing the approaches described in this book. With these processes in place, one can then focus on achieving the highest levels of marketing creativity and on adding more value through communications with customers.

Adrian Hosford,
Director, Customer Communications, British Telecom

Acknowledgements

We would like to thank all our colleagues in the world of direct marketing — agencies, client staff and consultants. They have contributed much to the learning which made this book possible. Particular thanks go to Adrian Hosford at British Telecom. His vision of quality in marketing communications has been an essential part of the experience which led to this book. Jill Parker, when she was at British Airways, Jon Epstein, when he was at American Express, and Carole Settachan of Unisys, also shared the vision of quality which this book represents. We also owe a great debt to Mike Wallbridge who, when he was at British Telecom, brought the two of us together as client and supplier, and initiated the development of a systematic approach to direct marketing, the results of which are demonstrated in this book.

Philip Mounsey
Merlin Stone

Part 1:
Principles

Chapter 1

Introduction

Many direct marketing books have been written. Some of them show the many different achievements of direct marketing and try to persuade the reader to do more of it, or take it up. Some help readers develop their use of particular direct marketing techniques (eg writing direct mail copy; lists; telemarketing). But this book is different. It assumes that the reader is already using direct marketing. It assumes a knowledge of basic direct marketing techniques. The reader may have his or her own customer database, or perhaps is building one. He or she may have a computer system which allows that database to be used to support direct marketing campaigns. He or she may be building such a system, or be using a bureau to hold the data. So what is left?

What is left is how to *manage* direct marketing. This means putting direct marketing skills to work through using management techniques. The combination of excellent direct marketing and thorough management will enable the reader to:

(a) develop campaigns which meet his or her company's marketing objectives
(b) deliver the campaigns on time
(c) measure and analyse the results
(d) continue to improve his or her direct marketing.

Company size

Where management practice is concerned, there are differences between larger and smaller companies. In a small company, direct marketing is often under the control of one manager. He or she usually works with a small agency and co-operates closely with the company's sales force or outlets. In larger companies this is less likely. Direct marketing involves co-ordinating a large team of people. Some of them, such as field sales staff or retail managers, may see the campaign as peripheral to their activity. Yet one's campaigns depend on them fulfilling their part of the campaign as professionally as if their jobs depended on it.

In-house work

In direct marketing a lot of the work in delivering campaigns is done in-house. This can surprise companies which are used to communicating with their customers mostly through media advertising (television, radio, press, etc). Large users of direct marketing have to manage relationships between many people, including:

(a) specialist direct marketers
(b) internal "customers" (eg product and brand managers, sales management, store operations management)
(c) systems staff (for the customer and other databases)
(d) a wide network of suppliers (direct marketing agencies, print production, telemarketing agencies, mailing and fulfilment houses, etc).

The "norms" of managing direct marketing have their roots in the practices of traditional mail order suppliers. These include publishers, general catalogue operators and speciality suppliers (eg collectables). Most of them have well developed management procedures for planning and implementing direct marketing campaigns. The same procedures should underlie direct marketing management in companies which have "real operations" (retail stores, factories, sales forces and branches). But managing direct marketing in such companies poses very different problems. These include problems of ensuring that the large number of people involved in direct marketing work together and produce quality campaigns and implement them in a quality manner. This book translates these procedures into a practical approach for any company using direct marketing as a key element of the marketing mix. It is not for companies who use direct marketing occasionally for the odd tactical campaign.

An art or a science?

In the world of direct and database marketing we like to believe we are at the more "scientific" end of the marketing spectrum. As far as possible, we distance ourselves from the image that the public associates with marketing — hype, buzz, inspiration. Advertising agencies may cry "eureka" when they hit on a big idea for a proposition. We, the direct marketers, are the engineers of the marketing community. We rely on careful campaign design, where targeting (who we communicate with) and timing (when we do it) are more important than the offer (what we offer customers) and the creative input (how we express the offer). Testing is supposed to be king, giving us the ultimate justification for our decisions.

We are supposed to work with a network of highly professional suppliers: direct marketing agencies, telemarketing agencies, mailing and fulfilment houses, printers, computer bureaux and a complex mix of media. These media are, in principle, carefully co-ordinated to achieve the optimum contact strategy — the succession of communications through which we induce our customers to buy and thereafter achieve the right levels of response and sales.

We are supposed to give all our suppliers careful briefings, well in time. This gives them plenty of time to interrogate the brief and ensures that everyone involved in the campaign understands exactly what we are trying to achieve and what they need to do to help us get there. We have clear lines of communication with them. This ensures that all parties know exactly the state of development of a campaign at any moment. When we launch the campaign, there is no rush. When the campaign is in the field, all resulting enquiries are handled professionally and swiftly, optimising customer satisfaction. When the campaign is over, we analyse carefully. We identify exactly which parts of the campaign worked best. This information on what worked is kept in a form which ensures that we can access it easily when we are deciding on future activity.

The age of process management

Or so we should like to believe! This picture is a utopian dream. But it is a dream which is slowly being translated into reality, not just in direct marketing. For many companies, the age of marketing inspiration was the seventies and the early eighties. We are entering the age of marketing operations management. This is the age of process management and attention to detail.

Most companies who are serious users of direct marketing are trying to be much more methodical about the planning and execution of marketing. This is also apparent in the management of other marketing functions such as strategic planning, product planning, distribution channel choice and management, pricing, marketing communications and selling. As companies are called to account for what they spend on marketing, they are realising that the relationship between expenditure and return in marketing does not depend just on innovativeness in marketing strategy. It also depends on professionalism of management in handling marketing resources.

When companies analyse how they manage their marketing they are often disappointed. It is then that they find out how weak their marketing planning is and how messy is their implementation, compared with the "paradigm" of the text book. Worse, marketers are realising that their management performance is much weaker than that of their brethren in other functions such as manufacturing and finance. The latter realised long ago that it is up to management to achieve quality in implementation.

Costs of poor quality

The consequences of lack of quality in managing marketing are readily identifiable. They include lost market share, high costs of late response to competitive challenge, or too high expenditures to achieve a given effect. Companies which have developed their own customer database and are switching a greater proportion of their marketing expenditure to direct marketing have been amongst the first to realise how serious these problems are. They often put the pressure on themselves. They sowed the wind of marketing accountability which justified so much database investment ("you will always know exactly what worked and why, because each response and sale can be traced back to particular marketing actions"). Now they are reaping the whirlwind, by exposing the general lack of management discipline in their marketing operations. Typical examples include:

(a) Late, incomplete briefing by "internal clients". This results in hurried campaign development cycles, poor targeting, rushed printing, unclear instructions, and the inevitable consequences of poor material or the wrong material being sent to customers, or responses being handled badly.

(b) Too aggressive objectives relating to database coverage. This leads to high volumes of low quality customer data being brought onto the database. This in turn leads to high mistargeting and returns rates, and high costs of database maintenance relative to financial returns.

(c) Lack of analysis of past results. This leads to poor targeting and wrong media choice.

(d) Lack of communication with those at the "coal-face" (eg field sales staff, branch workers). This leads to systems being developed which are cumbersome and difficult to use. It also leads to applications being developed in the wrong order (eg direct mail instead of telemarketing). This is because unless those who work at the coal face do their bit in "closing the sales loop", even the best laid campaign plans will not be realised. For example, a mail shot which produces a 20% response rate is no use if sales people are too busy to follow up the leads, or do not understand what they are supposed to do with them.

Investing in change

To overcome problems such as these, companies are investing in improving their management approach. They are investing in new marketing organisation structures, better planning and management skills, and improved information and communication systems. They are also trying to ensure that their marketers learn from the successes and failures of other companies. In some respects, we are seeing the maturing of the marketing discipline, as it moves from the "seat of the pants" approach into a "managed" approach.

This has important long term consequences. Many senior managers may not realise that marketing technicians (eg experts in branding, advertising, sales promotion, merchandising, direct marketing) may not be good managers. Marketers often criticise managers in other functions — personnel, production, and information systems seem to suffer the worst. But marketers' management shortcomings are among the best kept secrets of the trade.

However, all this is beginning to change. Leaders in direct marketing know that their investment in systems and database creation and maintenance will be wasted if it is not managed well. They are turning to well-established management disciplines to help bring method into what is potentially madness. Some marketers object to being compared, for management purposes, to research scientists, engineers and even construction workers. But others see the sense in using the management tools that have proved their worth in managing teams of people in difficult, uncertain and highly technical environments.

Project management

It is the sheer variety and complexity of direct marketing that creates the need for these management tools. Direct marketing usually involves running many campaigns a year. Each of these campaigns is a project. The problem with managing these projects is that each differs from the others. In terms of our engineering analogy, direct marketing is not a promotional production line, but a jobbing workshop. This workshop specialises in a particular range of products, each slightly different from the other. In producing these projects, the workshop uses some standard components, but has to custom-build many others.

To manage this kind of work, we cannot issue the same instructions over and over again. We have to customise our approach to each project. This is why we need to use project management techniques. These techniques are designed to progress complex projects through teams of people working on them. Our team may include specialist direct marketers, brand managers, sales staff, agencies and so on. They need to know what they are being asked to do. They need to know:

(a) how much they can spend
(b) what information they should be providing, to whom
(c) when they need to deliver results

and so on. Therefore, each promotional project must be properly planned, communicated, and delivered.

Projects and the marketing plan

The seeds of each project lie in the marketing plan. Once we have decided how we are going to deliver our marketing plan through direct marketing, we are in a position to start planning individual direct marketing campaigns. The direct marketer's job is therefore to create a series of campaigns. These campaigns must meet the needs of the company as a whole and the individual "internal customers" who hold the brief for specific products or markets. Each marketing campaign can be managed as a technical project. This is where the project management process enters. It requires:

(a) *The project file*
     We need a comprehensive project file for each campaign. It includes the relevant marketing plan details, forms for briefing all suppliers, the project timetable, sign-off authorities, criteria and codes for selections, descriptions and codes for all promotional material, forecast returns and actual results. A master copy of this file should be held by the campaign manager, and duplicates should be with all parties involved.
(b) *Project planning software*
     This is used to schedule the tasks required to deliver campaigns and reschedule them where slips occur. It is used to identify bottlenecks. It also produces status reports and enables us to identify accountabilities for failures.
(c) *Targeting and scheduling processes*
     We need management processes for targeting and scheduling campaigns. These reduce clashes and increase the effectiveness of targeting. The processes range from consensus to directive. The consensus approach may be through a team of all interested parties. The directive approach may be through a database directorate having authority to determine campaign

sequencing. In both cases, the company's in-depth understanding of the database and past campaign results should be deployed in determining which campaigns go forward.

(d) *Communication*

We need structured processes for communicating campaign status to all parties involved. In their most advanced form, these processes are computerised. In some cases, an extract from the campaign database is sent by electronic mail. In more advanced companies, all those involved in a campaign have direct access to relevant parts of a computerised campaign project file.

(e) *Training*

We have to ensure that marketers receive the management training they need to develop the skills their position requires. Typically, a specialist group of database/direct marketers, acting as both consultants and technical experts with authority to decide, needs training in:

(i) basic "consultative skills" — listening, communicating, influencing, interactive skills (meetings), contracting (fixing agreements)

(ii) how to put together projects that will meet customer needs and manage the projects through.

All these tools and techniques are covered in later chapters.

The systems aspect

Management lessons are also being learnt at the strategic end. As companies learn what is manageable, they are designing new systems and system extensions to be more manageable in practice. This does not just mean "user-friendly". At one time the focus was on the creation of the database and the gathering and maintenance of data. This is understandable because technology had just made possible the holding of large customer databases in a readily accessible way. But unless the database is used profitably, it is a waste of money. How it is used is determined by a combination of strategic priorities: what the company needs; operational necessities; what people at the grass roots level need to help them.

Many companies, knowing that they neglected many of their customers, created a customer database. They then asked their sales staff to keep in touch with more customers, using the database. Unfortunately, sales staff already knew who their best customers were and did not need help in dealing with them. The result was that the database was unused and its data fell into disrepair. Even sales staff who wanted to use it now found the data unreliable. The conclusion is to create a new team, properly selected, trained, motivated, targeted, compensated and managed. Give them the business of looking after neglected customers, entirely through the database, using telemarketing and direct mail. This conclusion is not very original. It is a simple case of ensuring that strategic priorities are translated into operationally feasible solutions.

We are seeing the same kind of phenomenon when it comes to campaign project management. Ask campaign managers to fill in a complex set of documentation for each project and they will do it under duress, probably scantily and in retrospect. They will not circulate it properly. They are right, because at the moment their operational necessity is created by a backlog of work. They deal with their work by decisions taken on the fly, abbreviated communication by telephone and fax, and crisis meetings. Creation of a structured paper-based process will not be welcomed by these people, although they may see the benefit. It creates more work for them and life is tough enough as it is.

Designing the management system

The answer is to ensure that the everyday reality of managing direct marketing is taken into account in designing management systems that are linked to the main database system. It is essential to have a system which will create most of the project file, communicating its contents to all who should know, watching out for slips and checking for clashes. This will ensure that campaign managers have *less*, not more work to do.

But here comes another management principle. If one expects people to change the way they work, give them time to do it, seek their input, retrain them and provide them with support before, during and after the change. There really is no such thing as a free lunch. A campaign manager struggling to deal with a backlog of work has *no* time to learn how to work a new system. He or she may need administrative support to help with data entry, checking and so on. Eventually, the ideal will be reached by these managers, with no backlog of work, and everyone knowing what they should know.

Today, few companies have achieved complete maturity in managing direct marketing. Several more are working towards it. They know that they must give themselves time to learn. They are also discovering that the principles of good marketing management apply across the board. Why should the campaign file for a sales force drive, an advertising campaign, or a major exhibition, be any different from that for a direct mail campaign? The techniques being developed for the management of direct marketing are already finding their application in other marketing disciplines, particularly those which involve a series of campaigns. This book is your guide to these techniques.

The structure of this book

The book has three parts. The first summarises key direct marketing concepts. We need to do this to make sure that we, the authors, and the readers, are on the same wavelength. The meat of the book is in Part 2, which covers the management procedures required to deliver according to the principles of Part 1. Part 3 covers how to keep it up, by ensuring that one is equipped with the right resources to do so! In more detail, the book structure is as follows.

Part 1: The principles

Chapter 2 covers planning. We show how to identify the implications of the marketing plan for direct marketing and how to determine what direct marketing can do. We develop the idea of planning a series of campaigns to achieve long and short term results, co-ordinating a campaign with other campaigns, and different approaches to co-ordinating campaigns, using a database and management information systems to support the planning process.

We also consider how to derive objectives from the marketing plan. We examine different kinds of objectives — brand loyalty, positioning, customer satisfaction, market defence and penetration, re-awakening of past customers, prospecting, reducing marketing costs. We discuss the objectives of relationships versus the objectives of individual campaigns, and how to combine the two.

Chapter 3 covers the basic elements of campaign strategy that are familiar to all direct marketers — targeting, timing, the offer, creative input. This chapter stresses the importance of understanding what has worked and what to watch out for in the light of experience. The choice of media to cover the target market is discussed here, as is the subject of media planning and how to improve the effectiveness of individual media. Some ideas about how to develop and narrow down options in campaign strategy are developed. Finally, we consider some ways to develop the database through incorporation of campaign-derived information, questionnaires and the use of lists.

Chapter 4 deals with the critical requirements for success in implementing your plans. It provides the bridge into Part 2.

Part 2: Procedures

Chapter 5 covers the need for a management process in direct marketing and outlines what that process should be. It leads into Chapter 6, in many senses the core of this book. This chapter provides the forms needed to manage each campaign properly, and a guide to their completion.

Part 3: Resources

Chapter 7 deals with supplier management. It is no use trying to get the best out of the wrong supplier, so this chapter deals with the many suppliers marketers may be using, and how to select, brief and manage them.

Chapter 8 deals with the team — recruiting, developing and keeping direct marketing staff, what to look for and how to organise, manage and train them.

Chapter 9 deals with what is needed in terms of management information systems to support direct marketing, and also covers some questions of how database development should be co-ordinated with marketing development.

Chapter 10 provides a comprehensive checklist, covering most of the contents of this book.

Chapter 2

Marketing Plans and Campaign Plans

Direct marketing is not a tactical discipline, although it has its tactical uses. A quality, high volume, properly managed campaign normally requires at least four months to plan and get ready for launch. In very large companies, using databases covering millions of customers, much database analysis may be required, followed by simulation of campaigns. Complex contact strategies may need to be designed and tested. In such cases the lead time may be six months or more. Faster campaigns have been run, with good results, but the norm for most companies is between three and six months. Trying to mount a campaign at too short notice almost invariably leads to quality problems. This is one reason why direct marketing campaign planning should be part of marketing planning. It should not be left until after the marketing plan has been published.

But there is a more important reason why direct marketing campaign planning and marketing planning should be part of each other. If companies are using direct marketing as a strategic part of their marketing mix, they cannot very well produce a marketing plan unless they have some idea of how they are going to be using direct marketing. If they use direct marketing as the only way of reaching their customers, there is no distinction between the marketing plan and the direct marketing plan. The marketing plan is in effect a series of direct marketing campaign plans, united by strong marketing themes.

So, campaign plans should be derived from marketing objectives and form an essential part of a marketing plan. Of course, marketers may not have all the details of every campaign identified when the marketing plan is finalised. But they should have a good idea of what kind of campaigns they will be running, when, with what coverage, costs and returns. The marketing objectives and the other marketing activities planned are important determinants of the type of campaigns marketers want to run.

The situation is more complex for the specialist direct marketer in a company which uses a varied mix of marketing methods and channels of distribution to reach its customers. It is even more complex if the company's marketing planning process is weak. The weakest marketing plans are just a compendium of the action plans of various product and sales groups. In these cases, marketers' campaigns may be the consequences of marketing plans drawn up by others, or in co-operation with others. Some of the campaigns they want to run may overlap with others targeted at the same market. This is why a management process for campaign co-ordination is needed.

If marketers are having co-ordination problems, their company will probably benefit from a proper marketing planning process. This is not just to remove the need for *ad hoc* co-ordination exercises. It is to ensure the deployment of all company marketing resources to achieve overall objectives and to stay ahead of the competition.

If marketers are not confident that their marketing plan provides them with the right framework for campaign planning, they may be in a position to create one or at least help their company create one. Below is what we would expect to find in the plan (summarised in Fig 2.1). In practice, many companies find that they only need some parts of it.

1. Executive summary

In companies with many products, operating in many markets and with many types of customer, marketing plans are complex. The result is that many people who should read the plan do not. If they do, they may not remember its details. A good management summary ensures that the dominant themes of the plan are expressed forcibly

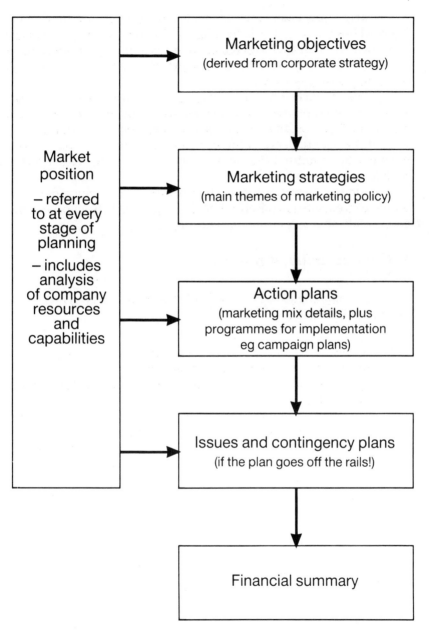

Figure 2.1 Marketing plan structure

and clearly. This means that no-one has the excuse that they do not know where the company is heading. The reader might be surprised to know how often this is given as an excuse. If the marketing plan cannot be summarised in a few pages, there is almost certainly something wrong with it.

Busy direct marketers love good executive summaries. Direct marketers are often professionals in their field. They know more about direct marketing than about their own company. A good summary is a vital aid to understanding company direction. It is also a very helpful attachment to briefs to direct marketing agencies (subject to confidentiality).

The summary should not, by its nature, go into much detail. It should concentrate on objectives, main target markets, opportunities and threats, and key strategies and timings.

2. Current market position

This is a comprehensive statement of where the company is now. It covers the following:

(a) how many customers the company has and what sort of customers they are (segmentation analysis)

(b) how many more customers it wants and where it expects to find prospects

(c) the buying behaviour of customers and prospects — what they buy, when and where, and in what quantities

(d) how much revenue and physical sales volume this behaviour results in, and the shares of different companies

(e) how these customers are communicated with. This includes their receptiveness to advertising, direct mail, telemarketing and other media

(f) who are the competitors and where are they going — their objectives and strategies

(g) what products are offered by the company and its competitors, their features and benefits

(h) the relative strengths and weaknesses of different companies and products

(i) how customers are reached — the distribution situation. Who sells what through which channel – sales force, agents, etc.

How business is generated for different products and segments through different channels

(j) macroenvironment situation — effects on markets of changes in the economy, society, legislation and regulation, etc

(k) summary analysis of strengths, weaknesses, opportunities and threats for the product/market *vis-à-vis* the competition

(l) the policies the company followed last year, and whether they were succeeding at the time the plan was written.

This situation analysis should provide enough information to indicate what opportunities are open to direct marketing. If this part of the marketing plan is properly produced, the kind of campaigns needed will almost stare the reader in the face. The most depressing situation to face is one in which the plan does not even identify the number of customers the company has, who they are and how much and when they buy. This means that much basic research needs to be done before the direct marketer can be sure that direct media should be deployed. However, if direct marketing is the company's dominant sales channel, much of the above information will have been produced from analysis of past campaigns.

3. Objectives

The objectives listed below should all be quantified. If they are not, it is very difficult for the direct marketer to transform them into targets for campaigns. They should cover:

(a) Market objectives — what the company wishes to achieve with its products, customers and markets. These include market share, sales volumes, market leadership, number of customers or users, frequency of use.

(b) Coverage — a precise definition of the coverage of the company's activities, ie target market (customer type, location, etc).

(c) Financial objectives — typically revenue and profit, whether absolute sums, margins or growth rates. Cost constraints will also be identified here.

(d) When these should be achieved by and what are the checkpoints along the way.

Objectives are often expressed hierarchically. Thus, the main objective may be a sum of profit. To achieve this, particular sales and profit margin objectives may be set. If direct marketing is the company's main sales channel, past campaigns will provide much of the evidence needed to ensure realistic targeting. It will show what profit levels and margins were achieved, for example.

4. Marketing strategies

These are how the company is going to achieve its objectives. Without clear strategic direction, direct marketers get very confused! They need to know the main thrust of their companies' marketing, as this determines the objectives and strategies for each of their campaigns. Strategy should cover:

(a) Branding — what values the company wants its customers to derive from individual products and from each product.

(b) Product proposition. This is the central idea that the company is trying to convey to customers for each product. It may be derived later as a result of work with agencies. However, we believe that treating proposition as an advertising issue is leaving it rather late. Surely, product planners should have some idea of the proposition, however clumsily expressed!

(c) Physical product features and benefits derived from them.

(d) Product positioning relative to competitive products and other products in the company's portfolio that might meet similar needs.

(e) New product development — what new products are coming.

(f) Capacity — how much of each product the company can produce.

(g) Developing usage by existing customers. This states what the company is planning to do to increase this. It may include cross-selling, to increase the range of the company's products used by any one customer.

(h) Development of customer relationship. This covers all the different relationships that exist between the company and its customers. It includes sales, marketing communications, customer service and other contacts. It identifies how these relationships can be improved to develop more business.

(i)   Customer recruitment — how new customers are going to be recruited.

(j)   Competitive attack and defence. This covers which competitors are going to be attacked, and how, and which competitors are expected to attack, and how their attacks will be parried.

(k)   Pricing — how much will be charged for different products.

(l)   Role of distribution. This covers which channels will be used to manage which customers.

(m)   Sales force — policy, training, remuneration, etc. If the company has a direct sales force, its proper deployment must be treated as a strategic issue. Otherwise, it will be left to tactical improvisation. This will certainly cause problems for direct marketing, which has to work with the sales force (eg in lead generation).

(n)   Marketing staff — recruitment, training, accountabilities. How the company is going to make sure that it has the right marketing skills to deliver the plan.

(o)   Customer service — how immediate relationships with customers who have bought the company's products will be handled, how their products will be serviced, and how the relationship so developed will lead to more business.

(p)   Marketing communication (advertising, PR, sales promotion, etc). This covers how different elements of the communications mix are to be deployed.

(q)   Use of marketing and sales information systems.

5. Action plans

This is the detailed part of the marketing plan, which takes strategies and transforms them into detailed actions at the level of who does what, when, how, where, at what cost, yielding what revenue and profit, etc. If direct marketing is the dominant sales channel, or very important in generating leads, then direct marketing campaigns will feature heavily here. The action plans should cover:

(a)   product introductions

(b)   details of changes to marketing mix (product, price, promotion, distribution — nature and timing of changes)

(c)   campaigns to be run

(d)   research and sales information required.

6. Issues and contingency plans

This covers any outstanding issues not dealt with by the plan and explores the likely impact of these issues, the main risks and ways of handling them.

7. Summary financials

This covers:

(a) projected profit, loss, cash flows and investment requirements, overall and for each product and market
(b) budgets for each activity
(c) phased plan — how financial requirements are split over time, to give budgets for each period.

If the plan is worked out in reasonable detail, and if the risks have been identified well, then developing campaign plans should not be too difficult (thought note that the need to co-ordinate campaigns may require a change in the timing of campaigns or modification to their objectives).

Planning the campaign

Ideally then, the marketing plan is where all campaigns should have their origin. If direct marketing dominates the marketing mix, then the section of the marketing plan that deals with implementation may consist of a summary of the direct marketing campaign plans. However, the relationship between campaign planning and marketing planning is not a simple one-way flow. In the process of campaign planning, marketers are bound to discover that some of the marketing plans were wrong. They may discover that some marketing objectives were too tough, others too low. They may find that for some markets direct marketing can play a greater part than they realised, in others that its effectiveness is lower than they thought.

The annual marketing planning cycle that most companies adopt makes it difficult to benefit from some of the advantages of direct marketing, namely:

(a) rapid learning from experience
(b) ability to test and then generalise to the whole market.

In a stable business, selling a fairly constant range of products to a given market, this disadvantage may not be too severe. Likely response rates and margins will be fairly predictable, so there will be few surprises. But this will not be so if markets are developing fast, or if the company is rapidly extending the scope of direct marketing, to include more of its existing products, and many new ones. In these situations, there is an argument for using a six month planning cycle. Much less would not be advisable, as the time from planning to implementation of strategic direct marketing projects is often six months.

If marketers feel that the relationship between marketing planning and campaign planning has not been properly thought through in their business, they must raise it as an important issue. We know that leading users of direct marketing have properly integrated the two approaches. In these companies, from the moment marketing objectives and strategies are conceived, the campaigns required to implement them are also conceived. In these companies, marketing objectives and strategies are determined in the light of past campaign results. Without this approach, people are bound to end up trying to use direct marketing to do the wrong things some of the time.

The campaign process

The process of developing and implementing each campaign should run through the following sequence:

(a) Planning — deciding how to meet marketing objectives through one or more campaigns, with specific objectives and target markets, promoting specific products and services, at particular times.
(b) Development — determine the details of each campaign.
(c) Implementation — running each campaign.
(d) Evaluation — analysing the results of each campaign.

This sequence is summarised in Figure 2.2. Let us look at it in more detail.

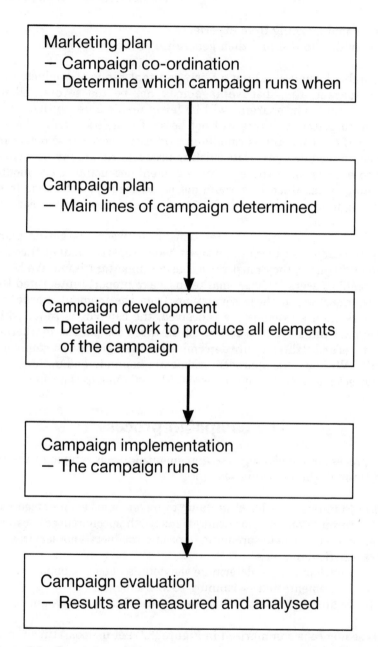

Figure 2.2 Campaign management sequence

1. Campaign planning

Ideally, the marketing plan provides clear overall objectives, strategies and targets. As we stressed above, these should have been specified taking into account the company's direct marketing capability. We are now concerned with translating the marketing plan into actions. If the company does not totally centralise its marketing communications, or if it operates through a variety of distribution channels, each with its own promotional programme, marketers must also ensure at this stage that their actions and those of others are co-ordinated.

For this reason we recommend that, as soon as possible, the campaign intentions are summarised in the form of an outline brief. This consists of the first five forms in Chapter 6, completed in as much detail as possible. This document, which we discuss in detail in Chapter 6, is effectively a summary of intentions — what the company wants to promote, when, to whom and how. In response to the marketing plan, marketers should produce a series of outline briefs and summarise them in the form of an overall plan of campaigns. Of course, they will also need campaigns to deal with unexpected problems or opportunities. But these tactical campaigns demand just as professional an approach as the more strategic ones.

Why not just produce a list of likely campaigns before going into the detail of outline briefs? In our view, writing the outline brief ensures that one knows exactly what one is planning to do. Without it, it is not possible to know which other campaigns a campaign will clash with. Therefore, marketers will not have a strong basis for determining campaign timings.

Obviously, the outline brief is refined and added to as the time approaches for initiation of more detailed work on each campaign. But by preparing the outline brief early and by circulating it to all parties involved (within the business and amongst agencies), marketers will ensure that clashes, data problems and resource bottlenecks are minimised and co-operation maximised. So drawing up and, where necessary, getting agreement to the outline brief should be undertaken as early as competitive and market conditions allow.

The brief is the key to well-planned and co-ordinated campaigns. It summarises the main details of the campaign. It also:

(a) helps organise thinking
(b) gives top-line guidance to implementers
(c) communicates the campaign internally and to suppliers
(d) is the supporting document for more detailed forms covering different aspects of the campaign.

Given this, many of the direct marketing procedures we describe later are tied closely to the outline brief.

2. Campaign development

This is when marketers put together all the details of the campaign (detailed targeting — including lists, timing, offer, creative input, etc), using agencies where appropriate. In this period the main concern is with getting all the details of the campaign right. This will ensure it runs smoothly once it is launched. Making sure all the suppliers are working well, to a common plan, and communicating progress, is a critical task in this period. The campaign documentation described in Part 2 will ensure that marketers do all that is necessary to achieve this.

3. Campaign implementation

This is when the campaign actually runs. Here, the major concern is likely to be ensuring that the logistics of the campaign are running smoothly (eg mailings going out on time, responses being handled properly) and that interim results are analysed to see whether any campaign details need modifying. This stage will normally be controlled through the customer database system and possibly managed through the management information system.

4. Campaign evaluation

After the campaign has run it is necessary to find out what worked and what did not. Here, the prime activity is analysis of response rates by different categories (media, market segment, timing of response). However, checking that the statistics were correctly measured is also important, to prevent false conclusions.

The rest of this chapter focuses on campaign planning.

Campaign planning

Setting campaign objectives

Above, we stressed the importance of starting with the marketing plan. The first step in relating the campaign process to the marketing plan is to determine which marketing plan objectives can be achieved through direct marketing. Below we list some kinds of objective, and the campaigns that might help achieve them.

(a) Gaining more business from existing customers

This can be done by:

(i) identifying, from purchasing data, whether there are gaps in the product and service range or variants, and creating relevant products and services, and promoting them

(ii) promoting existing relevant products and services to customers on the database

(iii) creating new relationships with existing customers, tying them more closely to the company and increasing customer loyalty

(iv) developing loyalty programmes, which allow customers to develop a closer relationship with the company

(v) identifying customers' requirements for levels of service, developing and promoting the required level of service, and following up afterwards to ensure that good service is remembered and less good service compensated for, to achieve higher levels of customer satisfaction and loyalty

(vi) identifying competitive threats to particular customers, developing stronger incentives for these customers and promoting them heavily

(vii) increasing the customer base, by developing profiles of existing valuable customers, applying these profiles to selected external lists, and promoting relevant products to customers so identified, and offering relevant relationships

(viii) re-awakening past customers, by identifying them, determining their needs, developing and promoting offers which meet these needs.

(b) Reducing promotional costs

This can be done by examining current methods of communicating with customers, and seeking to achieve the same effect through direct communication.

(c) Positioning and branding

If marketers want to support the creation of positioning and branding (master and sub-brands) with all customers, then maintaining strict standards in relation to the types of offer promoted and their creative presentation is necessary.

Examples of objectives

The objectives of specific campaigns might be to:

(a) reinforce brand loyalty
(b) achieve awareness of the company, of features, advantages and/or benefits of individual products, or of how to buy the product or service
(c) achieve product positioning
(d) convey a proposition
(e) demonstrate benefits
(f) customer satisfaction, eg draw attention to service benefits
(g) market defence, eg counter competitive promotion
(h) attack competition, eg promote to known users of competitive products
(i) market development, eg turn non-users into users
(j) get existing users to use more
(k) re-awaken past customers
(l) identify new customers amongst competitive and non-users
(m) reduce marketing costs.

The objectives form a critical part of the brief to the agencies involved in a campaign. If testing forms part of the campaign, or perhaps the whole campaign, the test objectives should be specified clearly.

One rule must always be observed — *keep campaign objectives simple and specific*. If the company wants to recruit good new customers, all its objectives should relate to this. It is necessary to specify what is meant by good customers, how many are wanted and by when. Objectives that are too complex can lead to a weak campaign.

The information required to justify the campaign is gathered from various sources which include the sales force, product or brand managers, market research and distributor sales. Most important of all, if the company has a mature database, is its analysis of responses and transactions data on the database. In the planning documentation, justification for the campaign must be given in terms of the main marketing objective that it supports (eg the need to increase sales of a particular product or to capitalise on a growth trend). The statement should be as specific as possible, particularly in terms of:

(a) the type of customer involved
(b) the attitudes and behaviour which we are trying to influence
(c) the influence of timing of customer behaviour on timing of the campaign (eg when they are most likely to buy).

This provides the key to campaign co-ordination, as well as setting clear, quantifiable campaign objectives.

Relationship objectives

If the company is using direct marketing strategically, then one of its strategies may be to use direct marketing to create a relationship with customers that transcends individual campaigns. This resembles how a salesperson develops a relationship with his or her customers that transcends the individual sale. Here, we learn from the experience of companies which have been using direct marketing for some time. Their most successful campaigns are part of a long term relationship with their customers. Developing this relationship should be one objective of the marketing plan.

Various themes can be developed during a relationship. Here is an example of development of a theme.

Stage 1 Recruit a set of customers (new or existing) into a new relationship.

Stage 2 Promote to them an offer which is relevant to the relationship.

Stage 3 Promote second and subsequent offers to them (cross-selling, or selling one of the products to users of another of the products).

Stage 4 Develop further offers based upon a study of those with the greatest take-up (more cross-selling).

Stage 5 Enrol customers in member-get-member programmes (in which existing customers recruit new customers).

Stage 6 Develop offers which group products together.

The development of a relationship can be over a short period (say six months) or over several years. In practice, very long term relationships should be composed of a series of short, feasible steps, paid for all along the way by the take-up of offers.

For example, to achieve objectives marketers may need to:

(a)   increase usage by existing users
(b)   motivate customers for the company's other products who do not use the product in question to start using it
(c)   make conquest sales from those who do not use the product but use competitive ones
(d)   attract totally new customers.

These tasks are arranged in order of difficulty. Earliest results are likely to come from existing customers (they have already demonstrated that they need the product). The slowest results will come from totally new customers. It may be possible to attract a few totally new customers as a campaign sequence begins, but achieving significant numbers (and getting them to stay with the company) is likely to involve a more concerted effort.

Quantifying objectives

Direct marketing requires quantified objectives. These in turn should come from the quantified objectives of the marketing plan. If marketing plan objectives are not quantified (at all or in enough detail), it is still necessary to quantify the direct marketing objectives. For example, they may be quantified in terms of net profit or return on investment.

Any objective set for a campaign should be quantified. What is more, the marketer should also ensure that the campaign plan includes details of how performance against objectives will be measured, whether through responses, actual sales or research measurements. The proposed quantification should include:

(a) target levels of achievement
(b) dates by which the achievement is to be reached
(c) for longer term campaigns, where there is scope for changing the approach during the campaign, interim measures, to show whether the campaign is achieving its target, and dates at which these measures are to be taken.

Campaign development

Campaign development covers the targeting, timing, offer and creative input. The media chosen should be a consequence of the targeting decisions and the nature of the offer the company wishes to make. Testing strategy is an important part of campaign planning and should be determined right from the start, in terms of what the company believes is important to test for its particular market, product, medium, etc.

Before beginning briefing, marketers should have a campaign plan already sketched out. This should not be set in concrete, as the agency briefing process is likely to lead to much refining of objectives and strategy. Developing the details of the campaign is the subject of the next chapter.

Chapter 3

Campaign Development

Campaign development is the heartland of direct marketing. It covers targeting and timing, combined into contact strategies using particular media, the offer and creative input (see Fig 3.1). The whole subject is comprehensively covered in all good text books of direct marketing. So in this chapter, we summarise the most important points. This is to ensure that we are talking the same language when we deal with the associated management process.

Integrated communication

But first — a caution. Many traditional direct marketing books focus on the application of targeting, timing, the offer and creative input to direct mail and, occasionally, the telephone. But we live in the age of integrated communication. Our aim is to deploy *all marketing communications media* together. Mail and the telephone work best when they are deployed in this way. For example, if one wants to create national awareness for a new product and then find customers for it, media advertising followed by direct mail may be the best way. In consumer markets, the combination of television, mail, retail display and telephone can be particularly powerful. In industrial markets, exhibitions and seminars combined with mail and the telephone can have similar power. But for these media to exercise this power their use must be planned and executed together. Because

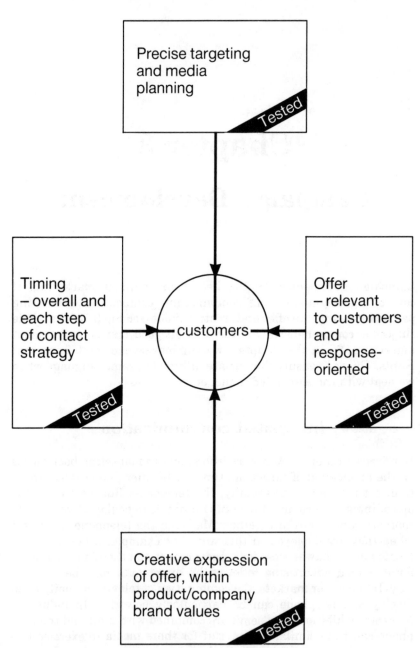

Figure 3.1   Main topics of campaign development

they are traditionally planned separately, special attention must be given to project-managing them together. Because much direct marketing methodology derives from direct mail practice, the integration of telemarketing is often weak. So marketers must take particular care to ensure that the telemarketing side of a campaign is properly planned, briefed and managed.

Marketers must be prepared to integrate the different concepts which are the traditional preserve of different marketing disciplines. The "proposition" and "key thought" used in the advertising campaign must be transferred to the mailpiece and to the telemarketing script for the three to work well together. In this way, the right "take-out" (what the customer will say about his or her contact with the company) and consumer action (what the customer does) will be achieved.

The concept of the managed dialogue, in which contacts between the company and its customers take place in a structured way, must be applied to media advertising. This becomes the "front end" of the dialogue – the incentive to the consumer to start the dialogue. As the dialogue continues, direct mail and telephone must be integrated with other actions, such as the sales call. (See *Telemanage your Customers* by Merlin Stone, Anna Thomson and Christopher Wheeler, Gower 1990, for how to integrate telemarketing with sales account management.)

Using so many media, marketers must watch the brand values which the company has so carefully built up. This means adopting clear rules on copy and presentation in every medium.

In this complex world of multi-media marketing the basics must not be forgotten. It is easy to be carried away and use different media to present different features of products. "Keep it simple" is still the basic rule. Present the products in terms of their benefits, in the language of customers.

Multiple results

Although the idea is to keep objectives simple, a multi-media campaign may have different types of effect on customers. It may affect loyalty, awareness, sampling behaviour, purchasing and so on. Although the prime measure of results should be profit, research is important. If a campaign is liked by customers, the research results should show that people think that what is being done is a good idea.

The results should show that they have felt involved in the campaign and that it will bring benefits.

But marketers cannot be satisfied with this alone. If they get into a serious dialogue with customers, they must be able to deliver practical benefits to them. This is what respondents are often after. For example, if one promises to save respondents time, one must show how.

If the campaign aims at changing attitudes, not just sales, it should be done in detail, for each target segment. The attitude change objectives should be set before the campaign, and attitudes must be researched before and after the campaign.

If the aim of the campaign is customer loyalty, it should be recognised that it is built over time. Once the company has it, there are many benefits, but it needs to work hard to get these translated into sales.

Differences in markets

The way the above should be implemented depends on the type of market one is in. In complex technical markets, try to present information for products in digestible chunks as part of the dialogue. Try also to emphasise product and service benefits for the individual as well as the organisation.

The more direct marketing one does, the more one will learn from customers. One's ability to segment will increase and different ways of approaching customers will be discovered. So be flexible. Adapt or modify the message as data becomes more detailed and needs change. Be different but always stay relevant.

Targeting

Targeting should be as specific as possible. With a clear statement of marketing objectives and strategies, marketers should be able to identify the customer types who form the target market for the campaign. Good targeting is a creative process, split into two separate and very different issues:

(a) to whom the campaign is being aimed
(b) how to find them and gain access to them.

Creativity is required in answering the "to whom" question, to determine the different customer types who fit into the target market definition. At this stage marketers try to (almost) forget such critical issues as whether they can actually identify these people. Instead, they use their knowledge of their customers to build a picture of the different types of person who form their target market. For example, the target market for a very high contribution executive pension plan might include directors of very profitable small businesses, directors of big companies and so on. The database should provide the ability to turn each of these definitions into different selections. Once marketers know that they can select these different types of customer, they can allocate resources to developing different, relevant promotional actions for each customer type.

If the database has been built over several years of promotions, marketers will be able to use another kind of creativity — the statistical. A variety of statistical techniques are available to help in identifying clusters of customers who are similar in one or more ways (eg usage of particular products, locations, interests). The higher the quality of the data, the more it will be possible to rely on this approach for creative targeting. Also, marketers will have fewer problems in finding and gaining access to identified groups. In this respect they will have an advantage over the traditional market research-based segmentation — the segments will by definition be on the database!

Incomplete information and the use of profiling

The customer database may be incomplete. Customer types may have been identified using variables on which data is held for only some customers. In this case marketers may want to use the technique of profiling. This involves taking the customer types identified and seeing what they have in common in terms of variables on which more complete information is held (eg location, age, income class). This profile can then be used as the criterion for selecting a large number of customers on the database. It is not possible to be certain that all those in the selection will have the right characteristics, but one can be certain that a good proportion will. Of course, to make sure, the profiling criteria should be tested by making offers to a sample of customers so profiled.

There will be many people on the database in the "prospect" category about whom there is little information. The information held on them may be "once off" information given when they responded to a questionnaire. It may lack the transaction information because they have bought the company's product through a third party channel of distribution. In this case it is necessary to identify links between the kind of data held on them and their purchasing behaviour, through customers on whom the company holds both types of information. Once this has been done, the usual profiling approach can be followed.

Defining target segments

Once the different types of customer the company wants to access have been agreed, the ideal is to try and make different target segments out of them. If the customer types were found through using the customer data, then the main problem is to determine what media to access them through. If they were found through other means (eg market research, brainstorming) it is necessary to match them to the customer data. Where the customer data does not provide the answer, it is necessary to search for media (eg external lists, advertising or promotional media) which will provide the needed quantity and quality of coverage.

Segment sizes

The *number* of customers in the target market should be determined by our quantified campaign objectives. In some cases, we may be targeting *all* customers in a particular geographical market who fit a particular definition. In other cases, we should have quantified sales objectives, which should lead through expected response and sales rates to a target number to be contacted. If sales volume to be achieved by the campaign is critical but we have no idea of response or final sales rates, then — if there is time — a test is indicated. Once again, a properly integrated marketing and campaign planning framework is a critical factor in making time for testing.

Contact strategy

The fine tuning of targeting leads naturally to the question of contact strategy and media choice. At this stage forget the detail. What marketers are trying to do is to offer different and creative ways for the individual to receive information and respond to offers. They may want to use a two-stage mailing to get the customers to segment themselves. They may want to invite their customers to call them so that they can telescreen them. They might want to use a questionnaire as a second step in the contact strategy, to help them fine tune the next step. Prospects who drop out are often uninterested anyway, but those who stay are moving towards the company.

Timing

Timing can be split into two elements:

(a) *Macro-timing* — when the campaign should be run. It takes into account other campaigns which the company might be running and the target customers' needs.

(b) *Micro-timing* — when each element of the campaign's contact strategy should be run. It takes into account the timing of other elements of the campaign and what the company knows about the likely receptiveness of customers at different times (of day, week, etc).

Macro-timing

Macro-timing is determined by the marketing planning work, which should lead to a co-ordinated series of campaigns. Obviously, a key part of the justification for any campaign is why it should run at the proposed time. A specific issue is frequency of mailing to good customers. This must be controlled, but also tested across different products. Evidence from many sectors shows that there is almost no limit to the number of times one can mail a loyal customer. However, one condition applies to this. Every mailing must be good quality, relevant and consistent with other mailings. The same applies to telephone calls, particularly in industrial markets. No calls must be idle. They must all be of benefit to both caller and respondent. If there is no policy on frequency, one should be developed and kept under review in the light of experience. Testing and customer research are required to monitor response and attitudes under different mailing frequencies.

If the company is selling many products to its customers, and its contact strategies have more than one step, the risk of overcontacting is even greater. Find out the optimum frequency by testing (for response) combined with research (to ensure no customer alienation). Although the company needs to optimise its use of postal discounts, the drive to do so should not be allowed to cause friction with customers.

Micro-timing

Micro-timing should be based on in-depth knowledge of customers' receptiveness to different types of communication and how different media work together. Information on this will come largely from past campaigns and from agencies, if they have experience in similar markets. The more one tests timings, the better position one will be in to know how to phase the different promotional actions that form the campaign.

Do not forget the usual direct marketing timing issues, eg:

(a) avoiding times when customers' attention is elsewhere (eg in consumer markets, just pre-Christmas) and focusing on times when attention is guaranteed (eg after Christmas)
(b) ensuring that the merchandise is ready to go out and able to be delivered. Avoid postal strikes!

The offer

The offer is not just a description of the product. It combines one or more propositions with incentive(s) to try the proposition. More than one proposition may be promoted in a campaign. However, certain media do not handle several propositions well (eg TV).

The areas to explore for propositions include:

(a) product characteristics — performance, quality of service, reliability, variety of functions
(b) market factors — types of customer, market share, exclusivity

(c)   ways of using the product — to save time, to make more profit, to treat oneself

(d)   surprising facts about the product, users or usage (used by celebrities)

(e)   price characteristics — value for money, money back guarantee, discounts

(f)   image — top quality, good value, friendly, reliable

(g)   needs-satisfying — physical, status, etc

(h)   company — nationality, energy, direction, customer orientation

(i)   disadvantages of non-use — what one loses or misses by not buying

(j)   competitive comparison — product, company

(k)   newsworthy — recent changes, anniversaries, topical events, new facilities.

All these propositions will be weak unless the customer is given a reason to respond and a date to respond by. This applies at any stage of any promotional action during the contact strategy. Sales promotion disciplines should be used to check the customer is being motivated all the way.

There are many ways of generating response through the offer. If a high quality response is required, the offer should be related to the product or service. For example, a free solar calculator may provide a high response, but the end result may not be good. However, if one is confident of the accuracy of one's targeting (ie the people one is communicating with are the right ones and are really in the market now!), one may want to "artificially" push up the response by a non-related offer. The offer that is most relevant to the product is normally value-added to the product itself or more of the product (eg two for one), with the "call to action" being a limit on the period of availability of the offer.

If one wants to be really sure which offer is the best — test. If there is not enough time to test, look at the results of past offers for similar campaigns (similar products, similar target markets). Some customers are mail-responsive, others telephone-responsive. Certain kinds of customer respond to certain types of offer, others to other types of offer.

Creative

In all forms of marketing communication, the creative element — the expression of the campaign in words (printed, broadcast or telemarketing scripts) and pictures — is always the most obvious and attracts the most interest from management. Despite this, and the apparent claim that it is not hard to get the creative side right, poor creative input is still a major contributory factor to delayed campaigns and last minute rushes. Worse, the scope for confusing customers through the form in which offers are put is also great.

Creative standards

Most big direct marketing users know that consistency in creative standards is essential. They have gone well beyond the introduction of standards on the portrayal of the corporate logo. They have clear standards on the layout of print, the look of pictures, the tone of copy and so on.

Branding

These standards are not monolithic. In companies with many products and divisions, the creative requirement can differ greatly. However if one aims to develop a long term relationship between the customer and the whole company (as represented by the master brand), then the master brand must come through in every presentation for it to be reinforced. Each sub-brand must have a clear relationship with the master brand. Rules for relating the two in every medium must be stated. If rules have not yet been stated for the medium with which one wishes to promote, then ensure that the master brand and positioning is not infringed upon by including clear statements of them in the brief.

Role of the brief

The brief is critical to good creative input. Many problems with the creative element which seem to be located in agencies can often be tracked down to a bad brief. Omissions which are particularly likely to cause problems include:

(a)   imprecise or too generalised a description of the target market
(b)   inadequate specification of how the buying process takes place
(c)   lack of clarity on desired tone, proposition and branding
(d)   inclusion of too many objectives for the medium being used
(e)   inconsistency of message and tone with the particular medium being used.

Different media are able to sustain different degrees of complexity of message. For example, in a mailing several pieces can be included, each with different objectives. Provided they are clearly from one company and have something in common, there should be no problems. This is because customers tend to look at each enclosure, which may therefore carry separate messages. But each enclosure should be single-minded. The portfolio approach is therefore allowable. The same does not apply to television or radio, where the same approach would cause customers to become very confused.

The above notwithstanding, the creative element should always go through the company's approval process to ensure that the master brand is properly supported.

Checking the creative element

We have included in Chapter 10 a comprehensive checklist to help readers check every aspect of a campaign. We have broken the checklist down into sections and advise readers to check each one separately. The section on the creative aspect should be studied particularly carefully. Marketers should also, as part of the briefing process, signal to their agencies which questions they must deal with successfully so that they know how they are going to be evaluated.

Promotional actions

The promotional actions marketers use for their campaigns should be as simple as possible and based on what they *know* works for customers in the target market. However, they should normally test any new approach, otherwise they will never give themselves the chance to learn.

Whatever promotional actions marketers choose, they should make sure that they know the objectives and expected results of each step.

This will ensure that everyone involved in the campaign knows exactly what to do or expect.

For each promotional step, specify:

(a) The objectives — what one wants to happen to customers who are the target of the campaign (eg be informed or persuaded, give information, identify themselves as being in the target market, ie hand-raising, buying a product).

(b) How one wants them to respond (eg fill in a questionnaire and send it, buy a product and give proof of purchase).

(c) How the promotional action will achieve this (eg description of mail-pack or advertisement, in particular the response device if any).

(d) How many customers one expects to respond in different ways.

How many steps?

Try to achieve a result in one step for each target segment. However, there are many occasions where two steps are needed. For example, if the aim is to recruit new customers, most of them in the target market may not be on the database. It may be necessary to use media advertising or external lists with a straightforward letter and small leaflet for identifying prospects. This might be followed up with a more expensive mail pack to those who have confirmed that they are in the target market. This might achieve a more effective contact (in terms of final results versus costs) than sending an expensive pack to the external list.

Media choice

In choosing media, use two sources of expertise:

(a) The company's database administration — to find out what has worked for customers in the target market. To do this, define the target market segments and ask database administration for a report summarising previous promotional actions and response details for that segment.

(b) The agency — particularly if the target segment is not on the database.

Narrowing down options

When the campaign has been drafted out in terms of target segments
and promotional actions, it may be found that too many possibilities
have been identified. If they are all followed, this can lead to high
promotional costs and poor results. At this stage the following questions should be asked:

(a) Do we need all the target segments that have been identified?
(b) If so, do we need to address them simultaneously? Is there
     scope for prioritising or for seeing whether the most important
     segments produce the right level of response?
(c) Are there economies in combining segments?

Getting the numbers right

The main reason for using direct marketing is to make more profit.
A few campaigns may be justified on other grounds, but unless it is
possible to show that the company is making a profit from the
activity, the use of direct marketing will be at risk. For this reason,
marketers should usually try to defray the costs of developing a
campaign over as large a target market as possible. Through testing
or experience with complete campaigns, marketers should try to
identify the rates of trade-off they are getting between response rates
(and sales rates) and campaign coverage. Too high a response rate
and too much contribution per promotional contact, may mean that
one has run too small a campaign. If the opposite occurs then the
campaign was too big.

The process for determining campaign size should go as follows:

(a) *Segment*
     Break down the target market into target segments
(b) *Costs and benefits*
     Identify the likely costs and benefits of promoting to each
     target segment. Distinguish fixed costs from variable costs
     and also what the effect of more precise targeting and more
     targeted offer design will have on response rates. If the benefit
     to the company cannot be stated in profit terms but the pro-
     motion is essential for strategic reasons, marketers may want
     to use what is called an "alternative cost" measure. This meas-

ures what it would have cost the company to promote to the customer using the next best method. The implication here is that the difference is being saved.

(c) *Lists*

If marketers have research which indicates that large numbers of their target market are not on the company's database, they should consult with their database administration or list brokers about which lists should be used. They should also consult with their agency about which advertising media to use.

(d) *Database analysis*

If large numbers of the target market *are* on the database, experiment with selections until:

  (i) several target segments have been identified which do not overlap and which differ significantly in the kind of offer that can be made to them.

  (ii) a simple selection criterion will suffice, because more complex selection criteria do not give target segments of sufficient size for marketers to cost-effectively and meaningfully promote to.

(e) *Selections*

Define the segments for selection purposes.

(f) *Measurement*

Make sure that all the criteria by which the success of the campaign will be measured are specified.

List usage

In choosing a list, whether to add to existing data or to get data on prospects not on the database, remember the following basic rules:

(a) the company's own database will give better results than external lists

(b) the best external lists will have customers that resemble the company's own

(c) a list of responders pulls better than non-responders (eg compiled) and a list of mail-order buyers pulls best of all (other things being equal).

Types of consumer list

Mail order purchase lists include fashion, gardening, household, book/record clubs, magazine subscriptions, holidays, investment/insurance, gifts and self-improvement. If a list is not available, try inserts in a publication that reaches the target market. Ideally, choose a publication which defines a strong affinity (eg a members' publication). But publications are often weak on customer profile definition, so accurate targeting is more difficult.

Lists of responders but not purchasers (enquirers, first step from two step sales, controlled circulation publication requests, exhibition attendees, life-style databases compiled from returned questionnaires) are usually less responsive but often offer a better ability to target.

Compiled lists (investors, professionals, electoral roll, etc) are less responsive but offer the best ability to target, being usually compiled as part of a data-gathering exercise. In business to business marketing, the job title may be better than the name, due to high staff turnover. Shareholder lists are a specially valuable category in the United Kingdom, because of privatisations.

To make a decision about lists, one needs to know the source and type of offer within the source. The source may be from a mail promotion, insert, media, readership/membership (controlled/paid), or compilation. Marketers may need a list broker's working knowledge of the list, not just the profile. This means knowing what works and what does not.

Marketers need to know frequency (how often customers on the list buy/respond), recency (when they last did so), amount (how much they bought) and category (what type of product they bought) of purchase. If the list is one of subscription expiries (this shows they have at least bought at some time in the past), it is necessary to know when they expired. It is also necessary to know who are the most recent purchasers ("hot-line") and how often the list is mailed to (the best are usually mailed most often, because they like receiving and responding).

Remember, although externally provided data may be very valuable, experience has shown that companies with established customer databases need to be very selective about what information they buy. Marketers should *always* test the usefulness of additional data, whether it is new names and addresses, or additional information on customers which is already on file.

Most lists marketers may want to use will be rental only, with a high degree of security. Samples of mailings may be asked for by the list owner. It is sensible to plan list usage well in time to ensure that one obtains the right coverage and quality for the right price. In particular, allow for the various data processing operations that need to take place before a list can be used.

It is necessary also to allow time for testing each list, otherwise money may be wasted. To test a list, the campaign needs to be large enough to test it against other sources of data to check that the variance in the result is due to the list. The recommended size of a list test cell is 5–10k for a first time test and 25–50k to validate. If the list is too small, a sample of the list should not be tested; test the whole list.

Testing

In direct marketing the best route to success is to find what works and to go on using it. However, one must still test to see whether one could have done better. Testing should be confined to the areas where it is believed the greatest return lies.

There are two kinds of test:

(a) on a sample of the target market, before full roll-out. This is often to test whether the targeting and media are right
(b) within a full campaign, usually with different customers receiving different offers or packs, to see which works best.

In nearly all campaigns there is ample scope for testing offers, media and lists. In all campaign briefs there should be a clear specification of what is being tested and what one wants to learn by testing.

The ability to test is limited by the fact that the expected response, size of test sample, significance level (the probability that our estimate is accurate) and confidence interval (the definition of the upper and lower limits of our estimate) are related. For example, suppose one is planning a campaign where the response rate is expected to be 4%. If we want to be 95% sure whether the result, if applied to the whole target market, will fall within the confidence interval of

3–5%, the sample size needs to be much larger than if we only want to be 90% sure that the result falls within the band 2–6%. What size is chosen depends upon the costs and benefits of the campaign. For example, if break-even is 1.5%, one may be happier with the second set of criteria, and so be happier with a smaller test cell.

What next?

All we have done so far could be considered the easy part of direct marketing. Once, this statement was not true. We genuinely did not know what worked best. With many years of experience in direct marketing now accumulated, most of us are confident that we know how to go about developing a campaign. The focus has shifted to implementation.

Chapter 4

Campaign Implementation

In most direct marketing text books the focus is on what marketers need to do out in the market to make campaigns happen. However, events in the market are carried out by people. Many of the deficiencies in campaign implementation result from mismanaging the people implementing the campaign. These include internal marketing staff, systems staff, agencies, mailing and telemarketing companies, fulfilment houses and so on. In this chapter, we set out some of the rules to follow to ensure that campaigns are implemented properly.

Project planning, scheduling and implementation

Once a campaign is given the go ahead, the process of implementation begins. The first step in this is to identify every one of the tasks which need to be done to implement the campaign. In Chapter 10 there is a list of all the tasks we have been able to identify. In Chapter 9 we have simplified them and arranged them as a project plan, showing where we believe tasks can be carried out in parallel. The project plan shows the kind of timings which should be allowed from the time that the campaign is given the go-ahead.

Tasks can be defined at different levels of details. The simplest is, of course, just *plan – implement – monitor*. We believe that planning should be at the most detailed level. But if this is difficult marketers should find some level which ensures that all the tasks they should carry out are performed and that their completion is communicated to the team. One approach is to focus on *major* milestones, which also provide good points at which to review progress.

Programming the campaign

One of the first steps which will normally need to be taken once the campaign has been planned is to translate it into systems language. This translation ensures that:

(a)   the right selections are made
(b)   details of customers selected are prepared in the right format
(c)   these details are conveyed to those responsible for outbound contact
(d)   files are prepared to handle response data and so on.

Entering the campaign details onto the system is therefore an important bridge between planning and implementation. How this is done in the company depends on whether the marketers (specialist direct marketers, brand managers, sales managers and so on) have direct access to the system. The kind of direct marketing campaigns likely to be run by most large companies are very complex, in terms of selections and contact strategies. It is quite enough for marketers to get the marketing side of it right, without expecting them to programme the main customer database system. The best that we can expect is for marketers to enter their *requirements* on a management system. This disciplines them to cover all eventualities. The forms in Chapter 6 can easily be handled by such a system. Although great advances have been made in database software and design in the last few years, we believe that it is more sensible to have a specialist database administration team. This team is responsible for both the integrity of the data and the integrity of campaign programming.

If the company has a good central team, they develop in-depth knowledge of the contents of the database, the selections that have been made from it and the results of campaigns run on these selections. Their knowledge and skills enable them to advise marketers on their targeting and contact strategy. In some companies, this central pool of expertise is reckoned to be one of the main marketing assets of the company — so vital that the team is given the authority to control access to the database. They are, so to speak, the custodians of the customer base.

In some cases, particularly in companies with a very varied product range and constantly changing priorities, it may not be possible to adopt this centralised approach. In this case, marketers may be given direct access to the system. The only restriction takes the form of a few basic controls to reduce the chances of misprogramming or campaign clashes. In this case, it is critical that they are properly trained. They must be given the chance to enter "dummy" campaigns. They should be encouraged to trial small real campaigns. Finally, they must be given support where they feel they need it.

Making the project plan happen

It is one thing to plan a promotional project, another to make the plan happen. Much of the work involved is not in one's hands, but in the hands of external suppliers or other staff outside one's control. Imposing a plan on them without consultation is unlikely to produce results. Other parties have to agree that what one is asking for is feasible. Therefore, a draft plan should be drawn up and discussed with them.

Please note that the two major causes of promotional projects departing from their agreed timetable are:

(a) lack of communication
(b) lack of attention to detail.

Communication covers everything from clarity and comprehensiveness of brief, and communication of the project plan to provision of speedy and clear feedback at every review stage. It is, therefore, essential to *allow enough time for communication.*

Attention to detail means not letting anything slip. The annals of direct marketing are filled with examples of coupons going out without media coding or return addresses, the wrong fulfilment packs being sent to the wrong customers, the wrong telephone numbers being publicised, campaigns going out before telephone response handlers have been trained, and so on.

The implementation forms which are provided in Chapter 6 are designed to ensure that every aspect of the campaign is communicated to the right parties, while the task lists and checklists of Chapter 10 are there to ensure that marketers do check every aspect of the campaign before approving it.

We recommend that marketers complete these implementation forms as a natural part of organising their work, while the task lists and checklists should eventually be carried round in their heads.

Likely problems

Problems in promotional project management are of several kinds:

(a) it is difficult to meet deadlines
(b) suppliers have the same trouble
(c) the quality of suppliers' work is lacking.

Most of these problems stem from the same origins, typically:

(a) not identifying all the tasks required to take the project through to completion
(b) not knowing how much time each will take or not allowing the time
(c) not allocating the tasks clearly among the different parties (the company's staff, different suppliers)
(d) not briefing people clearly or being asked to respond to an unclear brief, particularly when there is no time to clarify it
(e) slack budgeting.

None of these problems are peculiar to direct marketing. Other areas of marketing and selling have their own horror stories. Most of the above problems are likely if not enough time is allocated for developing and delivering the campaign. The more hurried the campaign, the less time there will be to *manage it properly*. We believe that if marketers follow these steps they are less likely to experience problems:

(a) Pre-brief planning should be done thoroughly, so that one is totally clear on campaign objectives, strategies, accountability and timetable.

(b) When planning it is essential to communicate and consult. Ensure that all relevant parties have agreed that the objectives, plans and timetable are feasible.

(c) Do not confuse customers. The company's communication may be one of a series received by customers — whether direct or through the media. It is necessary to position the company's offer not only relative to the competition but also relative to other offers contained in its own communications, so that customers understand where the offer "fits" relative to the others. Also, make sure that customers know exactly what the company wants them to do. Otherwise they will call all sorts of people in the company and it will be impossible to handle many of the responses the company is so keen to get.

(d) Complete the master brief (Forms 1 to 5) well in time. Where appropriate, submit it to database administration early enough for them to comment, suggest modifications and prepare to meet its requirements.

(e) Complete the rest of the planning forms as soon as possible, and circulate them to all parties (internal and external) who are working on the campaign.

(f) Work out the timings for each step of the project plan and get them agreed with any collaborators.

(g) Identify important milestones, manage by them, and get all collaborators to do the same, making sure that they (especially agencies) have got the right management process and discipline.

(h) Measure progress towards campaign launch and learn from the experience if things do not go according to plan.

(i) If suppliers do not understand the process by which the company works, brief them and if necessary train them to use it.

(j) As elements of the campaign start to emerge (eg the target list, the mailshot), use the appropriate section of the checklist to check them off. This will guarantee quality.

Project timing

In Chapter 9 our simple project plan provides an example as to how much time should be allowed for each activity in the promotional project. This is based on an analysis of past promotional projects in several companies. We have produced it by passing the data through a computerised project management package, which allows us to take into account the effect of dependencies of activities on each other, and which activities can be undertaken in parallel.

If the company's system does not provide this facility, but marketers are happy using microcomputer packages to organise their work, they should ask their systems people to provide them with one and to help them use it. This will be particularly useful on complex promotional projects where they anticipate slips and changes in priorities, or where they have to run many promotional projects at once. This approach will enable marketers to be more closely in control of their projects, and manage any problems if slips occur.

Monitoring and control

Direct marketing works through measurement. Measurement during campaigns helps marketers to check if their strategy is working. Measurement after a campaign enables them to find out what worked and what did not work. In setting up a campaign, marketers need to make sure that the right information is reported at the right time to the right people (ie those who are in a position to do something about it). This means:

(a) Deciding what key performance indicators they wish to use. They must, of course, be measurable as well as useful.
(b) Making sure that these indicators are actually measured. Ideally, they should not require special measuring techniques, but be picked up as a normal part of the campaign.
(c) Making sure that the results are communicated to the right people.
(d) Ensuring that the actions indicated by these results are taken.

Control information

The information needed is fairly straightforward and derives from the logical flow of a campaign. Below are some examples. Note that many of the measurements are simple checks on the volume of flows (of communication) or stocks (of material to be communicated). The measures are as follows:

(a) For where the first communication is direct, the number of customers actually selected by the selection criteria (or the number of valid names on a list).

(b) Availability of stock of initial mailing material, checking that numbers match selection/list numbers.

(c) Volumes actually dispatched and timings of dispatch.

(d) For where the first communication is through broadcast or published media, that the advertisement or insert was according to schedule and that the right number of people actually received it.

(e) Numbers responding to the first communication and categories of response.

(f) Availability of response packs.

(g) Response pack mailings — timing and volumes (applying to every subsequent action step).

(h) Results of response pack mailings (category and timing) eg sales.

The flow rates of outbound and inbound communication are very important. They are the key to checking inventory of mailing material. The inbound rates are also critical in forecasting the final result, but obviously can only be understood if we know when the relevant outbound step took place.

Information sources

The above information comes from many sources. Where it comes from suppliers (eg media buying, mailing, response handling), part of the contract with them should be the supply of high quality, up-to-date statistics. Many companies new to high volume direct marketing have had significant problems in this area. These can easily be avoided by attention to detail at an earlier stage. Failure to get these statistics from suppliers means that at any one time no-one knows exactly what the status of the campaign is. Provision of these statistics should not only be part of the conditions of the contract with suppliers, but also specifically detailed in the brief for each campaign. Most of the problems in this area are caused by campaign sponsors failing to specify their requirements of suppliers in enough detail.

In detail, each supplier should be told:

(a) the data required
(b) the frequency of reporting
(c) procedures for signalling problems.

Contingencies

Marketers should consider contingencies for where results are not as expected. Examples include where:

(a) responses are too low or high
(b) problems emerge with stocks of mailing or fulfilment material
(c) media schedules are altered for reasons beyond marketers' control.

For example, if response is too high, fulfilment pack stocks may run out. Can additional stocks be ordered quickly (this needs to be established during initial negotiations with suppliers), or can a later wave of outbound communication be deferred? Before taking a snap decision, however, the reason for the high volume needs to be established. Was the outbound mailing larger than expected? Was there a special reason why more people than usual might have seen the press advertisement? Has there been a high volume of responses from "friends and family" as well as from the target respondents?

The same applies if response is too low. The achieved media schedule should be checked. So should the selection criteria or list used. Perhaps there were delays in the outbound communication. Were all the components of the pack included? Did the right response packs go to the right respondents?

The statistics that one receives are an important line of defence in ensuring quality. Let us assume that the right selection criteria, lists or media have been chosen, the offer has been designed well, and implemented through appropriate creative means. If so, then the control statistics tell one how well internal and external suppliers have been organised, and how well they have observed the brief. Analysing control statistics over several campaigns will provide a good idea of whether there is a fundamental problem in a particular area. For example, does a particular mailing house always mail out late, or does a fulfilment house always notify stock figures too late? Has one's absence on business or holiday caused problems in the management of a campaign, suggesting that a sharing arrangement with colleagues would help?

The problem with learning after the event is that by then we are on to the next campaign. Control statistics are forgotten. So they should be kept, ideally in simple graphic format, as a permanent record of the campaign's progress. This will help to review, for example, the performance of particular agencies over several campaigns, or to evaluate one's own judgement.

Learning from final results

Monitoring and control during a campaign are closely related to final evaluation, except that during a campaign we usually evaluate basic flows and stocks (responses in and packs out); after a campaign we are typically evaluating rates and ratios (eg profit per contact).

There are many ways to measure a campaign's effectiveness. Some are non-monetary (eg response rates), others are cost ratios (eg cost per response, relative media cost productivities). In the end, the most important results are customer satisfaction and brand support, and how these are translated into financial measures such as revenue and profit. We can use intermediate criteria to judge effectiveness. These are based on the chain of productivity — the ratios which determine the relationship between input and output. A simple example of such a chain is:

(a) profit = unit profit × number of units sold
(b) number of units sold = sales per response × number of responses
(c) number of responses = responses per customer reached × number of customers reached.

Using intermediate measures, the campaign could be evaluated by:

(a) the number of customers it reaches
(b) how many responses it generates (of each type)
(c) the number of bookings made
(d) incremental profit from the campaign

(e) how much it increases customer lifetime value
and so forth.

Each campaign must be evaluated against other types of campaign as well as in conjunction with them. Thus, we might evaluate mail versus telemarketing, each medium covering customers with a high propensity to respond to that medium, and mail versus telemarketing, covering all customers. We should also evaluate mail with telemarketing as a combined contact strategy.

The "cost productivity" statistics we use to judge the effectiveness of different campaigns include:

(a) cost per 1000 mailed or per phone call
(b) cost per decision maker contact
(c) cost per lead achieved
(d) cost per sale.

These should be compared for different media. The cost of different elements of the sales process (outbound contact, enquiry handling and fulfilment, concluding sale) should also be evaluated. These should be set against revenue and margins achieved (including any selling of products which were not the subject of the promotion).

Quality statistics should also be accumulated. These include database quality statistics (eg gone aways) and measures of the quality of the response handling process (eg average elapsed time before fulfilment pack sent out).

Building the database value

If marketers are responsible for a clearly defined sector of the market, then they also need to evaluate long term performance across several campaigns. This requires some simple modelling of the customer base of the kind normally carried out in mail order companies. We have included such a model in Chapter 9. This can help marketers to evaluate the benefits of recruiting a particular group of customers onto the database. It also helps them plan the frequency of campaigns. An immense amount of statistical experience is built into such models. The more experience marketers have with their database, the better the position they are in to develop such a model.

The process

Much of the content of this chapter may seem a tall order to the average beleaguered direct marketing manager. The answer is that without a proper management process he or she has not got much hope of making all this happen. Even if he or she does succeed once, it will be necessary to work just as hard next time to make it all happen. This is where management process comes in.

Part 2:
Procedures

Chapter 5

The Management Process for Implementing a Campaign

Many direct marketers have to design and deliver campaigns without any management process. Some are given as guidance a list of "stages of campaign development". This was fine in the days when direct marketing consisted of the odd tactical campaign. Today, when direct marketing has become central to the strategic marketing of many companies, it is not good enough.

In certain companies the need for some kind of process has been discovered during a quality programme. Here, every department is asked to specify:

(a) what its purpose is
(b) who its suppliers are
(c) who its customers are
(d) how it identifies and delivers against customer requirements
(e) who is accountable for what and when.

In other companies, the need for a process is discovered as a result of serious failures to meet standards, whether deadlines or campaign quality.

The kind of process required depends very much on the type of company and how it organises its marketing. What follows are detailed suggestions as to the kind of approach which might be adopted and the information requirements of that approach.

Why a process?

What are the benefits of having a process? A good management process brings benefits in the following areas.

Resource allocation

It allows resources to be allocated based upon a clear understanding of the future workload of every member of the team. This improves resource utilisation and the quality of work carried out. This is especially needed in direct marketing. Direct marketing departments tend to commit to a large number of campaigns before working out whether they have got the time and resources to do the job properly.

Management support

It provides management support to members of the team, including suppliers and internal customers (eg brand managers, sales managers). Direct marketing is a very detailed and information-intense activity. At every stage of a campaign many decisions have to be made and much information is needed. A good process ensures that the right information is available at the right time to the right people. In particular, information on the status of campaigns is readily available.

All this reduces the time wasted looking for information. It reduces time spent in meetings exchanging information. Meetings are expensive and should make the most of the "brain-time" of those involved — discussing options and making decisions. A good process has the added benefit of identifying problems earlier. It also reduces the time staff spend on sorting out administrative complexities and improves morale.

Supplier management

A good process improves the management of suppliers. This starts with supplier selection and continues through briefing and quotation, to tracking of suppliers' work. This in turn enables suppliers to work more effectively with the company's team. The team can manage its suppliers more tightly, leading to budget savings. This is because a good process identifies when supplier inputs are required and ensures the time is set aside to deal with them. These inputs range from quotations and negotiations to actual delivered work.

Lead times

A good process improves lead times, allowing time for better, more cost-effective implementation and for more pro-active management of opportunities. This is rather chicken and egg. Initially, implementing a process may increase lead times as the team gets used to working with them. But eventually, because campaigns are managed more efficiently, they can be managed through to completion more quickly.

However, this does *not* imply that briefs can be left until later. The benefit of an improved process should be taken through increased quality of campaigns, not quicker turnaround. Indeed, we are arguing for campaign development cycles which are on average *longer* than in most companies. We would like to see the campaign development cycle begin earlier, at the latest as soon as the marketing plan is drawn up. With campaigns well managed and properly paced, one can then deal with urgent campaigns more speedily, while maintaining quality.

Campaign quality

This covers all the key elements of a campaign — targeting, contact strategy and media; timing; offer design; and the creative input. The right information is provided to the right person at the right time. Accountabilities are clearly allocated and milestoned. The whole campaign will be managed better and produce better results. This is likely to be visible first in avoidance of mistakes, and later in better results.

What is a management process?

A management process is simply an organised way of going about things. More simply, it is a statement that when we do X, we do it this way. The elements and visible signs of a process include the following:

Planning and decisions

Analyses	Task planning	Problem resolution
Progress chasing	Progress management	Meetings

Information handling and reporting

Regular reports	Exception reports	Communicating progress
Review cycle	Output evaluation	Result publication
Enquiry handling	Notifying requirements	Computerisation
Form filling	Data entry	Documentation
Filing		

Resource processes

Budgeting	Resource allocation	Negotiation/influencing

People processes

Role definition	Accountabilities	Motivation
Management action	Staff appraisal	

There are many ways of viewing how a process works. One way of describing a process is according to the length of work cycle that is managed by it. We have found the following distinction useful:

Day in the life— the everyday job of managing work. This includes filling forms, data entry, filing, diary management, back-up provision and meeting management. The focus here is on individual tasks and balancing between them on a daily basis. At the human level, the focus is on such things as checking that matters are proceeding according to plan, managing problems, helping people complete tasks, supporting and giving them lift through motivation.

Month in the life — this relates to slightly longer term activities or projects. It includes putting together plans, implementing campaigns, briefing suppliers, recruiting, developing, communicating with and motivating staff, measuring performance.

Year in the life — major activities and very important projects. These include launching a major new product, development and implementation of a strategic campaign, production of a business-wide plan. Also included here are longer term activities relating to people eg appraisal, long term development, promotion.

Running a process

Some processes can be self-administered. This applies particularly if tasks are simple and routine and all involved know what the tasks are, why they are necessary, and the consequences of not doing them. Self-administered processes also work well if managers concentrate on managing the exceptions. They should be by strong positive reward for successes *and* for working to the process, and negative reinforcement for staff not observing agreed processes. Self-administration usually consists of following a checklist.

But if tasks are not simple or required only occasionally, if understanding about the need for them is not widespread, then a hands-on approach to management may be required. In some cases a document-intensive process may be used to ensure that people work professionally.

Processes and procedures

"Process" and "procedures" are related. "Process" describes the general way one wants to deal with tasks. "Procedures" are the detailed steps involved in running the process. If a process and/or set of procedures is to work, these conditions must hold:

(a) Staff must understand and be committed to the process.
(b) Roles must be allocated clearly and staff must understand

them — eg what they are accountable for, what they can decide or influence.

(c) Staff must have the skills to carry out the roles and the time and resources required to do so.

(d) The process should produce clear benefits for staff, eg help them work better, reduce tension or conflict, give them clear standards by which to judge their own performance.

(e) Staff commitment to the process must be reinforced by management action (via involvement by management in implementing the process, setting clear priorities, administering rewards and sanctions). Appraisals must take into account contribution to the process.

(f) Management must know when someone is or is not carrying out their role, otherwise individual reinforcement cannot take place. In other words, managers must keep their ears to the ground!

(g) The objective of the process must be "right for the business".

(h) The process must be designed to support that objective or allow staff to work more effectively to achieve it.

Computerisation of the process

Ideally, most elements of the management process should be computerised. This applies particularly to planning, information preparation and distribution. In Chapter 9, we discuss how to computerise the management process.

Process description

A campaign process description constitutes two main elements, as follows:

(a) a step by step description of how a campaign will be handled — who will do what and when

(b) a specification of the data and communication requirements required to support the flow of work.

Campaign handling process

We have insisted that campaign planning should start when marketing planning starts. In practice, many direct marketers feel that
their company's marketing plan lacks the basis for this approach. It
may be too general, lacking the detailed objectives they require. Or
it may be produced too early and be irrelevant by the time it is
applied. Or it may be produced too late. If we were to recommend a
process which depended totally on the existence of a properly documented marketing plan, our ideas would be dismissed as irrelevant
by half our readers!

So, in what follows, we describe how we believe campaigns should
be handled — irrespective of the state of the marketing plan. A good
marketing plan will help marketers handle campaigns better. But it
is possible to develop and run good campaigns without a proper
marketing plan, provided marketers are professional in their
methods. However, if the company does not give the right support to
campaign planning, marketers must develop their own. If they do
not get clear guidance on objectives and priorities they must develop
their own approach. What follows explains our view as to how it
should be done.

Cross-campaign planning and co-ordination

The first point to recognise is that unless all marketing communication is based on direct marketing, it is necessary to co-ordinate
direct marketing with other marketing communications. One's
approach to this will be influenced by how one is organised. If direct
marketing is undertaken as part of the work of an overall marketing
communications department, then planning and co-ordination should
be organised for all campaigns, not just direct marketing ones. The
aim should be to co-ordinate all messages.

If direct marketing is managed in a separate department, then
direct marketers face the same problems that we mentioned above in
connection with the marketing plan. If there is an overall marketing
communication plan, well and good. Provided it is produced at the
right time and in sufficient detail (and with direct marketers' input),
the framework required is present. If not, marketers owe it to themselves professionally at least to manage their work properly.

Campaign planning and co-ordination is not theoretically complex.

It is just a question of making sure that campaigns deliver messages whose content and timing is co-ordinated and which contribute to the development of the company's brand(s). This means co-ordinating every aspect of campaign development. But different processes are required to do this.

Co-ordinating targeting, contact strategies — media and timing

In direct marketing this is mainly a question of selections (or lists) and when to use them. In companies whose main marketing channel is direct, such as mail, and which have good customer databases, co-ordinating selections is the key activity. This is so important that some companies treat access to the database as the most important marketing decision. Brand managers and sales managers are required to submit their briefs to the database manager. His or her job is then to determine who are the best prospects for the campaign in question and when they should be addressed. In deciding this, he or she takes into account the targeting, timing and offers of other campaigns.

In some companies the database manager suggests which campaigns should be run and what contact strategies they should use. He or she moves from being a gatekeeper of the database to the initiator of campaign ideas. This is because, through analysis of the database, he or she can determine what campaigns are required. The database manager plays the customer-advocate, with customers speaking through him or her on the basis of what campaigns they have responded to, and what campaigns are missing.

Offer co-ordination

In companies where a considerable investment goes into producing the product, and where direct marketing is a central sales channel, co-ordinating can be difficult. The company's need to run the campaign can clash with its need to run campaigns for similar products at the same time. As direct marketers, we have to accept this. The earlier the warning we get about the need to promote a particular product, the more time we get to develop ways of presenting products through offers.

Where the products differ greatly in their nature and target market, co-ordination is not a problem. But where products are similar, with overlapping target markets, we must develop ways of positioning products relative to each other. We need time to test how far the target markets actually do overlap, so that we can separate out the non-overlapping segments and promote differently to overlapping and non-overlapping segments.

Offer co-ordination depends on our having a deep understanding of target markets and product benefits. The secret of offer co-ordination lies in early briefing on product benefits, clear and early-stated views on target markets and decent warning of the required timing of campaigns.

Organising co-ordination

Many companies organise their co-ordination by committee. Incoming briefs are collated and submitted to a campaign co-ordination committee. This meets regularly (typically monthly) to review all briefs and slot them in. In other companies a planning department receives all briefs and allocates them a budget and timing slot. Whatever approach is used the most important achievement is getting briefs submitted in good time. But marketers must also ensure that the output of the planning process is properly communicated, so that the whole team knows what it must do and when.

Campaign statuses

Because it genuinely takes time to decide whether and when a campaign should be run, it can have different statuses, from being a gleam in the idea of a product manager, to being finished. It is essential to recognise this in the process. Here are the kind of statuses that a process needs.

Provisional

The campaign has been identified as needing consideration but has not yet been submitted for formal consideration by the campaign co-ordination process. Normally a deadline for such consideration should be set. The campaign proposal should contain an outline brief, timing and suggested budget.

Submitted

The campaign has been formally submitted for consideration through the campaign co-ordination process, with the brief and timing firmed up. Again, a deadline for approval or otherwise should be set.

Approved

The campaign has been approved by the campaign co-ordination process, with timings for development, launch and close agreed.

Budgeted

Although an outline budget should be considered when a campaign is at earlier stages, we believe that marketers should not budget until they have received quotes from suppliers. There is no point in getting detailed quotes before the campaign is approved, because this wastes suppliers' time and may slow down other projects. The outline budget should be based on experience with earlier campaigns. An outline budget also prevents time being wasted if suppliers think the requirement is not feasible within the outline budget.

Under development

Serious work has started on the campaign, suppliers have been briefed and money is being spent!

Live

The campaign has hit the market.

Completed

The campaign has been completed, as no further actions in the market will be undertaken.

Closed

The results of the campaign have been analysed and properly documented.

The above statuses are "operational" statuses. They describe what point a project has reached in its normal process of development.

However, things do not always run so smoothly. Campaigns may be cancelled, deferred or even absorbed into other campaigns. So we need four further statuses, as follows.

Current

The campaign is at one of the above statuses and progressing normally.

Cancelled

The campaign will not go ahead. This may be determined at any stage until the campaign is live. Marketers should keep records of the work done for the campaign, as it may be needed later.

Deferred

The campaign is deferred until later. No new timing has been specified and it will require submission through the co-ordination process.

Absorbed

The campaign has been absorbed into another one.

We call the above four statuses "management statuses". Changing a management status has important resource implications and may have legal or contractual implications with suppliers. For example, cancelling a campaign may create a risk of breach of contract with suppliers.

The different statuses are summarised in Figure 5.1.

Benefits of formal campaign statuses

If you observe these statuses, then it becomes much easier to manage campaign co-ordination and resource allocation processes. The whole team, including suppliers, will know at any one time what campaigns the company is considering, planning, working on and finishing. Figure 5.2 shows the type of display one gets from a management system when one works with such definitions.

If one computerises the approach to this, it is not too difficult to ensure that proper documentation on campaign status is maintained and circulated. More of this later.

Provisional	Approved	Budgeted	Under development	Live	Completed	Closed

Operational statuses

Current	Cancelled	Deferred	Absorbed

Management statuses

Figure 5.1 Operational and management statuses

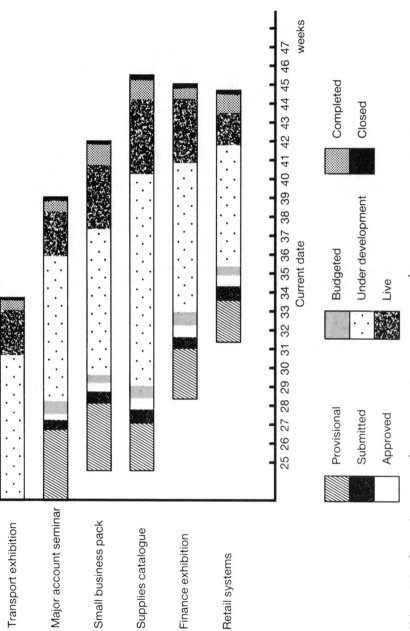

Figure 5.2   Campaign status chart – computer company example

Authorities

Who is responsible for making the decision at each stage and managing the campaign depends on how one is organised. Here is our suggestion as to how it might be done.

Provisional

The person initiating the request (the brand or product manager, sales manager, service manager, database manager, etc) is responsible for providing an outline brief, requesting timing and likely budget.

Submitted

The person initiating the request is responsible for submitting the campaign, unless there is some more formal process of allocating the progression of projects.

Approved

The manager of the campaign co-ordination process is responsible for making this happen. Any revisions to the brief, especially targeting and timing, agreed during the process should be circulated by him or her.

Budgeted

This depends on how one is organised. If the company's promotional budgets are centralised, then this may be the responsibility of the financial controller. If budgets are allocated to internal customers (eg brand managers), then they may be the appropriate authority.

Under development

The campaign manager is finally responsible for all work during this and the next two stages, live and completed, and for documenting the results at campaign close.

Cancelled, deferred and absorbed

The manager responsible for the last stage a campaign reaches is responsible for maintaining data on it. However, we believe the data should be centralised with the manager responsible for campaign co-ordination.

Staffing

One of the most neglected aspects of direct marketing management is recognition of the different roles that need to be carried out to ensure that campaigns are delivered properly. We have already discussed some implicitly — the campaign manager, the manager responsible for co-ordination. But there are other roles that management must fulfil. These include:

(a) initiation or origination — coming up with the ideas for campaigns

(b) workload control — ensuring that the resources of the team, including suppliers, are adequate to meet the demands upon them, and that work is scheduled so as to optimise use of these resources

(c) campaign administration – ensuring that all campaigns are correctly documented and communicated, and that everyone in the team meets their deadlines

(d) delivery — actually doing the job of bringing the campaign to market

(e) sponsoring – providing the funds

(f) being the internal customer — the person benefiting from the campaign, typically a product, service or sales manager.

In some companies, all these roles are combined into the job specification of the direct marketing manager. But in very big companies doing a great deal of direct marketing, the roles are often split. The most under-rated of all these functions is, in our view, campaign administration. Although quite a junior person can fulfil this role, we believe that a good campaign administrator is worth his or her weight in gold. How these roles come into play is described in the following section, which describes a typical campaign process.

Campaign process details

In what follows, we describe what should happen at each stage and who should do it. In order to do this, we need to refer to the information provided in some detail. Our approach has therefore been to organise the information required during a campaign into a number of forms, which should be completed as the campaign progresses. How marketers use this is up to them. We believe that without properly documented campaign files marketers are likely to commit more errors of commission and omission than otherwise. With the information properly organised they will at least have the basis for quality.

The forms, which are detailed in the next chapter, are as follows.

1. *Campaign definition and accountabilities* — describing the requirement in brief and saying who is involved in delivering it — staff, suppliers and internal clients.
2. *Campaign coverage* — testing and market coverage issues.
3. *Objectives and strategy* — where the campaign fits in overall marketing and promotional strategy and what it needs to achieve.
4. *Product or programme detail* — what exactly is being promoted and what its features and benefits are.
5. *Market detail* — to whom the campaign is directed, what their perceptions are, who the competition is and what they are offering.
6. *Campaign elements* — the detailed requirements of the campaign.
7. *Initial estimates* — what the company thinks the campaign is going to cost and what revenue it expects.
8. *Management and media timing plans* — the main milestones in campaign planning and above the line media.
9. *Mail and telemarketing timing plans* — the main milestones for direct marketing media implementation.
10. *Formal agency quote* — what the agency believes it should get!
11. *Outbound list selection brief* — which specific customers the company wants to target.
12. *Internal list selection brief* — as 11 but for when the database is organised into lists.

13. *External list selection brief* — as 11, but for when it is necessary to rent lists.
14. *Contact and fulfilment strategy* — what to do with each group of customers targeted.
15. *Contact and fulfilment details* — how to do this in detail.
16. *Contact strategy diagrams* — a diagrammatic representation of 14 and 15.
17. *Data — format and delivery* — how marketers want the data to be provided by the database system.
18. *Reports* — what reports marketers want from the database system.
19. *Systems feedback report* — how many customers have been selected by the selection criteria.
20. *Outbound telemarketing* — detailed brief to the telemarketing agency for outbound calling.
21. *Enquiry management/inbound telemarketing* — as above, but for inbound.
22. *Questionnaire summary* — to record details of questions asked in telemarketing or mailshots.
23. *Media — broadcast* — brief to media buying for TV and radio.
24. *Media — press* — brief to media buying for press.
25. *Fulfilment pack summary* — details of contents and suppliers.
26. *Fulfilment letter summary* — details of letter.
27. *Print production and distribution* — handling of printed items.
28. *Print delivery advice* — to ensure print gets to the right place.
29. *Campaign close report* — the results!

Process sequence

(a) As early as possible, the person initiating the campaign works out its main lines, completing as much of Forms 1 to 7 as possible, ideally after discussion with the direct marketing people. The status of the project is provisional.
(b) When he or she is ready, the initiator submits these forms through the campaign co-ordination process. The status is now submitted. The manager responsible for co-ordination checks what other campaigns are planned, and also checks the details of the submission with the initiator and the direct

      marketing staff. The campaign is agreed to be either approved, cancelled, deferred or absorbed.

(c)   If the project is approved, marketers should confer with the initiator to confirm the main elements of the campaign (Form 6) and submit Forms 1 to 6 as a brief to suppliers. During the process of their response, marketers receive quotes from them (Form 10) and firm up timing plans (Forms 8 and 9).

(d)   Marketers collate the quotes, negotiate with suppliers and arrive at a final budget. A budget is requested from the sponsor. When the budget is accorded the campaign is budgeted. There may be one or more rounds of negotiation before this is achieved. If no agreement is reached, the campaign may be cancelled or deferred until budget is available or absorbed into another campaign to achieve economies.

From now on, the sequence depends on how marketers work with their suppliers and their systems people. The timing plan should be as specified in Forms 8 and 9.

(e)   The direct marketing agency works out with the marketers the right targeting, timing, offer and creative input for the campaign. The marketers firm up on selections (Forms 11 and 12) and any lists (Form 13), and document the contact strategy and media (Forms 14 to 16). At this stage they may be negotiating with mailing and fulfilment houses. This gives them the information they require to specify how they want the customer lists delivered (Form 17) and when they need reports (Form 18).

(f)   The systems people tell the marketers how many customers the selection criteria have selected (Form 19). The criteria are revised if necessary.

(g)   The telemarketing agency is briefed (Forms 20 and 21).

(h)   All the questions used in telemarketing and mailshots are properly recorded, so that systems staff know how to handle them (Form 22).

(i)   The media brief is issued (Forms 23 and 24).

(j)   Fulfilment pack and letter details are recorded (Forms 25 and 26) as are print production and distribution details (Forms 27 and 28).

(k)   The campaign goes live and reports are received as specified. When the campaign is over, results are documented (Form 29).

Campaign administration

The above may seem a rather complex set of actions, but it represents what goes on in most companies, albeit often verbally or "on the back of an envelope". All that we have done is to rationalise it. If marketers implement such a process, they must work to a clear set of administrative procedures. Here is our suggestion:

(a) A master file must be maintained by the person given the responsibility for campaign administration.

(b) The file physically documents the process, but the process itself consists of management decision and action, followed by documentation.

(c) The files must be properly packaged, with clearly marked sections, so absence or incompleteness of any form can be detected.

(d) Some forms will be completed gradually, often as part of the response to an earlier stage of briefing. According to how one organises oneself, certain items of information should be mandatory by certain stages.

(e) Each form has one or more "principal recipients" but will be copied to all the team. All will have a copy of the file and its contents, updated each time a change is made.

(f) Whenever a change or addition is made, this is an amendment. The relevant sheet should be issued with a revised date.

(g) The summary of the response to each brief (where appropriate) is also kept on file. Suppliers must produce simple summaries for this purpose (no more than one page).

(h) As outputs of the earlier part of the process emerge (eg draft copy, graphics) they must be circulated to all suppliers by each supplier.

There are obvious benefits in computerising such a process. Without this, running the process will be very cumbersome. In particular, reporting will be very slow and paper-intense. The kind of reports that will need to be issued include the following:

(a) projects at different statuses
(b) date each form was last updated
(c) milestones due and missed

(d) budgets allocated
(e) quotes accepted
(f) data missing
(g) results summary
(h) work loading on staff.

Individual campaign reports should be filed with campaign documentation. Many reports will be across-campaign and may be the subject of departmental review meetings. Reports can also be used to track the performance of particular suppliers, brand or product managers, and direct marketing staff.

To make it easy to keep a campaign running to schedule, it makes sense to develop standard memos covering the transition between different statuses, chasing on milestones, and cover notes for reports and form updates.

On very big projects it is useful to properly automate the communications and computing side of communicating with internal customers and suppliers, through a name and address database and the installation of direct links into the department's systems.

Managing resources

If marketers run a large direct marketing department, then they need to ensure that the workload they are asking their people to carry out is feasible. Even though they may plan campaigns in a co-ordinated way, they will probably find that priorities change and work may begin to bunch. They may need a process for identifying where bottlenecks are likely to occur so that they can change priorities or deploy resources differently.

One approach is to install a production process. This views the department as a sort of jobbing workshop, through which campaign work progresses. Each "job" requires certain resources to progress it and each resource is required for a certain amount of time. If all the company's campaigns are organised using the kind of status descriptions we have used above, then it should be relatively simple to organise the production planning. The key question is how much each campaign takes of the different resources at the company's disposal. These might include direct marketing managers, print specialists, database and systems people, media planners and so on.

The production planning process reviews the forward workload with these aims:

(a) to check that the workload required of each resource is feasible
(b) where the workload of any individual or department is temporarily too high, to arrange for the redeployment of resources or the hiring of external resources on a temporary basis
(c) where the workload of any resource is permanently too high, to arrange permanent redeployment or increased resources
(d) where budgetary constraints prevent resource readjustment, to recommend that work be deferred or ended.

The planning horizon used depends on the average period from the time a campaign is identified as likely to run, to the time it goes live – its gestation period. This is likely to be at least four months and may be up to a year. We believe that the planning period should be at least double the gestation period.

Information requirements

To plan properly, marketers may need to bring all their planning information together periodically, typically every few weeks. If they run their campaign co-ordination by a monthly meeting, then it makes sense to have production planning on the agenda. To make sure that the meeting does not waste its time, the following information should be circulated beforehand:

(a) the status of all projects under gestation or live
(b) the likely loadings of all these projects on different members of staff and agencies. It is not easy to estimate these, but marketers should be able to do it in half day units
(c) likely bottlenecks, particularly situations where staff are dependent on unreliable external events.

If it is found to be hard to estimate the time that staff need, the agency idea of time sheets may be found to be useful. These can be abused if they are used for client-billing purposes, but may help staff trying to manage their time. If there is a problem of staff managing their time poorly, then the use of time sheets might be introduced alongside a time management package.

Figure 5.3 # Time planning sheet

Four week period ＿＿ to ＿＿.
  Enter half-days likely to be spent on each activity for each individual.

	Staff 1				Staff 2				Staff 3				Staff n				TOTAL			
Week no.	1	2	3	4	1	2	3	4	1	2	3	4	1	2	3	4	1	2	3	4
Campaign 1																				
Campaign 2																				
Campaign n																				
Managing staff/ being managed																				
Campaign meetings																				
Other meetings																				
Other (specify)																				
TOTAL																				

If it is decided to use time sheets, it should not be forgotten that it is necessary that staff enter all the time spent on non-campaign activities. Their time sheet should then be summarised on a departmental sheet, as shown above (Fig 5.3).

The forms

These are the focus of the process because they carry all the information needed to manage each campaign. In the next chapter we present and describe each form.

Chapter 6

Campaign Forms

The forms provided here serve three purposes:

(a) To help plan and implement a campaign. The forms help to do this by ensuring that every bit of detail that a direct marketing campaign typically requires is covered.

(b) To provide a basis for formally briefing others. If marketers work out the detail correctly and use the form to make a record of it, then they have created a clear basis for communicating their intentions to others on the campaign team. The very act of planning creates the campaign file.

(c) To communicate marketing plans clearly. Apart from those on the campaign team, others need to know what is being planned. Creation of a master file using these forms makes this easier to do.

The first five forms include all that a direct marketing brief normally covers. Forms 6 onwards cover the detailed work involved in implementing a campaign.

We believe that the first five should be mandatory as part of the process for translating the marketing plan into campaign plans. If the marketing planning process is weak, then these five forms give enough information for decisions to be made on campaign priorities by whatever body makes them in the company (eg a campaign co-ordination committee).

These forms may seem rather bureaucratic. However, all the information they cover has to be written down somewhere and communicated to someone. The forms merely provide a systematic way of ensuring that all planning, briefing and communication actions are carried out. Our experience is that unless all the details of a campaign are specified, it is very likely that something will go wrong. Nearly all the forms constitute either a brief or a response to a brief. The later the order of the form, the further downstream in the campaign development process it is used to brief or respond. For example, the later forms brief fulfilment houses, telemarketing agencies, printers and distribution centres.

The responsibility for completing each form is likely to vary according to how each company is organised. In some companies, the responsibility for all the forms might be best allocated to a specialist direct marketer. In others, perhaps less centralised, a product manager may be responsible for the earlier forms, and a direct marketing assistant for later forms. It is necessary to make sure that *every* form has a defined person responsible for its completion, and that there is *one* person responsible for maintenance of the master file.

It may not be necessary to use every form, or every section of each form, for every campaign. Some sections may be irrelevant for a particular campaign. Some of these forms may need modifying to suit a particular purpose.

Ideally, the forms should be computerised. This not only makes it easier to complete them, but also allows us to analyse the data in the forms. Approaches to computerising are discussed later, in Chapter 9. However they are computerised, we recommend that they are customised first and then tried out extensively on paper.

The recipients of copies of forms are determined by the details on Form 1, which gives accountabilities.

There is no rigidly fixed sequence to the completion of the forms, as some may be completed in anticipation. If the company is weak at planning, marketers may find that at first they end up completing the later forms before the earlier ones! However, in principle, the order should be roughly as presented.

Filling in the forms

Entry on all the forms

The following four entries are made at the top of each form:

Campaign title: The formal name of the campaign, eg Launch Mailing for Product X, Customer Loyalty Campaign for Small Business Spring 199X.

Campaign code: This would be the company campaign code. It is essential that a permanent system for campaign coding is instituted. This will be the coding that is used on the main customer database system to refer to the campaign. If the company has not already invented a system, it may help to choose a coding system which has a meaning, rather than a simple series (eg numeric, alphanumeric or alphabetical), where codes are taken in sequence. Marketers may want to code for market sector, product promoted, type of objective (eg product launch or customer loyalty). However, if the marketer runs a large number of campaigns, for many products and targeted at many sectors, a "rational" coding system is likely to become cumbersome. In this case, a simple series might be better.

Originator: This is the name of the person who completes the form in question. Who this is will be determined by how the company allocates responsibility for initiating and managing campaigns. If the approach to direct marketing is centralised, the originator for the first few forms may be the direct marketing manager. If the direct marketing team works with other marketers on a customer-supplier basis, the marketing manager requesting the campaign will be the originator. However, later forms, which concern the details of direct marketing, are more likely to be originated by direct marketing specialists.

Date of issue: When the last version of this form was issued. As a campaign evolves, it is likely to go through many changes. If the campaign team starts to operate from different versions of the same form, disaster could strike. It may be necessary to create a separate form, showing when each form was last updated, and circulate it with the campaign documentation.

Where additional material is needed to provide justification or support the information on any form it should always be attached. The forms aim to force communication and precision but cannot substitute for the much greater volume of information needed to brief suppliers and manage campaigns through.

Then follows the campaign description.

At the end of this chapter, we have included an example of how the master briefing forms might look when completed.

FORM 1: CAMPAIGN DEFINITION AND ACCOUNTABILITIES

CAMPAIGN NAME _____ CODE _____

ORIGINATOR _____ DATE OF ISSUE _____

DESCRIPTION OF REQUIREMENT _____

_____

_____

PLANNED LAUNCH DATE _____ PLANNED CLOSE DATE _____

MEASUREMENT CRITERIA _____

_____

CAMPAIGN MANAGER _____ INTERNAL CLIENTS _____

_____

_____

IMPLEMENTER'S NAME   IMPLEMENTER WORKLOAD

_____ _____ DAYS BETWEEN _____ & _____

_____ _____ DAYS BETWEEN _____ & _____

_____ _____ DAYS BETWEEN _____ & _____

_____ _____ DAYS BETWEEN _____ & _____

_____ _____ DAYS BETWEEN _____ & _____

SUPPLIERS

COMPANY   CONTACT NAME   OBJECTIVE/ROLE OF COMPANY ON
                              CAMPAIGN

1. _____ _____ _____

2. _____ _____ _____

3. _____ _____ _____

4. _____ _____ _____

5. _____ _____ _____

6. _____ _____ _____

7. _____ _____ _____

8. _____ _____ _____

9. _____ _____ _____

OTHERS ON CIRCULATION LIST FOR ALL CAMPAIGN DOCUMENTATION
(keep to minimum)

_____ _____

_____ _____

Description of requirement

This gives a brief description of the campaign (but fuller than the name!). It should include statements on size, target market and offer, and refer to any wider campaign of which it is part. Thus, our campaign above, Loyalty Campaign for Small Businesses Spring 199X, might be described as:

> Campaign to raise the loyalty of our top 3000 small business customers to product range Y, as part of our competitive defence strategy.

Campaign timing

This gives the start and end dates of activity in the market. It does not include planning time, but states the period during which direct marketing activity on the campaign will be taking place in the market. Obviously, the end date may be difficult to determine, as responses can flow in over a long period. Each company is likely to have its own convention for officially "closing" different kinds of campaign.

Measurement criteria

This gives the criteria by which the company will measure the success or failure of the campaign. It is placed very early in the form because the success measures will determine the whole approach to the campaign.

Campaign manager

This is the person formally responsible for delivering the campaign. Who this is depends on how the company organises its direct marketing, as discussed above. However, in most companies it is likely to be a specialist direct marketer.

Internal clients

If direct marketing works on a customer-supplier basis with other marketing staff, this is where the "internal clients" are specified. Marketers should indicate which ones have sign-off authority at which stages.

Implementer's name

In very big companies, with large direct marketing departments, there may be a senior direct marketer, to whom several more junior direct marketers report. While the senior manager may formally be responsible for the campaign, more junior managers might be involved in implementing it. In the case of very big campaigns, more than one may be involved. In this case, their names will need to be stated, as this form defines the campaign team. In addition, the senior manager may want to estimate the likely workload of each person, to ensure that they are not overloaded. The form gives the opportunity to specify workload. If the system is computerised, this will enable the senior manager to measure the total hours required across all campaigns for each junior manager. The days entered are *not* the total length of the campaign, but the total time, expressed in days, the individual needs to complete their part of the campaign. Ideally, a standard should be developed, eg half a day for briefing suppliers, six days for managing campaign through, two days for liaising with suppliers.

Suppliers

This section gives the company name, contact name and objective or role of company on the campaign, for each supplier. This is the basis for mailing all documentation and reports, as well as identifying the complete campaign team. As further suppliers are involved, it will need to be updated, by the campaign manager.

Objective role of company/department on campaign

This gives the role of each supplier on the campaign and has the same status as the above entry. This list will be added to as the campaign develops. An example of an entry would be "handling of outbound mailings".

Others on circulation list for all campaign documentation

This will be added to as necessary by the campaign manager.

FORM 2: CAMPAIGN COVERAGE

CAMPAIGN NAME _____ CODE _____

ORIGINATOR _____ DATE OF ISSUE _____

TEST OR ROLL-OUT _____

OBJECT OF TEST _____

_____

IF TEST, ROLL-OUT STRATEGY _____

_____

_____

_____

COUNTRY/REGION INVOLVEMENT

COUNTRY/REGION   TYPE OF INVOLVEMENT

1. _____   _____

2. _____   _____

3. _____   _____

4. _____   _____

5. _____   _____

6. _____   _____

7. _____   _____

8. _____   _____

9. _____   _____

10. _____   _____

Test or roll-out

Whether the campaign is a test or a final programme.

If test, roll-out strategy

If the campaign is a test, then this states what will be done with the results. There are several kinds of test. The company may be testing whether the target market offers the right response. Or it may be testing which market is the best. Or the target market may be given and the company wants to find the best offer for it. For a test of the offer, the statement might be "Test mail followed by pack against straight pack mailing, roll out one which produces best response". If the test is of targeting, the statement might be "Test in target market. If very successful, roll-out within six months, if borderline, modify and re-test, if very unsuccessful, scrap". Each of these criteria (eg very successful, borderline) should be defined.

Country/region involvement

In very large companies, campaigns spanning many countries or several sales branches or retail outlets may be run. If so, it should be clearly specified what coverage the campaign is to have. Just as importantly, the role of staff located in the countries or regions should be specified. For example, they may be involved in processing leads or even carrying out mailings.

FORM 3: OBJECTIVES AND STRATEGY

CAMPAIGN NAME _____ CODE _____

ORIGINATOR _____ DATE OF ISSUE _____

OBJECTIVES OF MARKETING STRATEGY OF WHICH CAMPAIGN FORMS PART

1. _____

2. _____

3. _____

4. _____

MAIN ELEMENTS OF OVERALL MARKETING STRATEGY

1. _____

2. _____

3. _____

4. _____

PROMOTIONAL OBJECTIVES

1. _____

2. _____

3. _____

REQUIRED CONSISTENCY WITH OTHER CAMPAIGNS AND ACTIVITIES

1. _____

2. _____

3. _____

DESIRED CUSTOMER RESPONSE

1. _____

2. _____

3. _____

PROPOSITION — key issue/offer from prospect's point of view

_____

_____

PREVIOUS PROMOTIONAL ACTIVITY TARGETED AT THE SAME

AUDIENCE _____

_____

Form 3 summarises the objectives and strategy of the campaign. The direct marketing agency will need to know this to be able to develop the right creative approach and contribute to the development of the campaign. This information also helps the company to determine campaign priorities.

This and the next two forms help marketers summarise the marketing context of the campaign. It will help them to brief the direct marketing agency and will serve as useful supporting material for campaign co-ordination work.

Objectives are the "what", and strategies the "how", but a high level "how" is a "what" for someone else, so the definition is relative. For example, to achieve the objective of more profit, the strategy of relaunching a product may be chosen. The promotional objective might be to achieve specific tasks involved in relaunching the produce.

Examples of objectives might be to achieve particular levels of awareness, volume of enquiries and/or actual sales of the relaunched product. The strategies to achieve these objectives might be to target promotions to attract new users, to cross-sell to users of another of the company's products, or to promote as part of a broader package. Objectives should always be quantified, so that we know whether the campaign is likely to be a good investment (and afterwards, whether it was).

Objectives of marketing strategy of which campaign forms part

These should come directly from the marketing plan, which should provide the objectives and strategy for all campaigns. These should be quantifiable and quantified, eg to increase sales of a particular service by 10% to £25m per annum.

Main elements of overall marketing strategy

This should cover the marketing strategies which the company's marketers are planning to use to achieve their objectives. Direct marketing will only be one part of this for most companies. This information is important for the agency, which needs to know what other marketing activity will take place for the product or service.

Promotional objectives

These are based on the marketers' assessment of the contribution that direct marketing can make to achieving the marketing objectives. For example, to increase the sales of the service mentioned above, the direct marketing contribution might be to generate leads for the sales force, in which case this would be the promotional objective. The number of leads should be specified, and this should be one of the measurements. Interim objectives and measures, such as the number of enquiries required, should also be specified.

Required consistency with other campaigns and activities

This indicates how far the campaign needs to "fit" creatively with other campaigns targeted at the same audience, and how far direct marketing needs to use ideas employed by other types of marketing communication targeted at the same customers (eg TV advertising, packaging). Normally consistency with master branding goes without saying in many companies, but at this stage it should be stated, as well as other kinds of consistency (eg same tone as previous campaigns for Brand X). Timing issues should also be mentioned (eg avoid proximity to promotion of Brand Y). Consultation with colleagues during planning and analysis of campaigns already planned should ensure that marketers have solved the consistency problem. This form ensures that marketers communicate the situation to all involved in the campaign, particularly agencies.

Desired customer response

This describes what we want the customer either to take out from the campaign or to do. This is important for the direct marketing agency. It should be clearly tied to measurement criteria. Examples of this include: to visit store X, to sample product Y, to buy service X.

Proposition

The key issue/offer from the prospect's point of view. This might be set before the direct marketing agency is briefed. However, the marketers may brief the agency to develop the proposition. An example would be "Try our product X before (date) and you will find that it makes doing Y a lot more pleasant".

Previous promotional activity

If the customers targeted for this campaign have received other promotions recently, these should be specified, to ensure consistency and avoid clashes in messages. This information may be available from the customer database.

FORM 4: PRODUCT OF PROGRAMME DETAIL

CAMPAIGN NAME _____ CODE _____

ORIGINATOR _____ DATE OF ISSUE _____

PRODUCTS/SERVICES/PROGRAMMES TO BE   CODE
PROMOTED/OFFERED

1. _____ _____

2. _____ _____

3. _____ _____

4. _____ _____

5. _____ _____

PRODUCT OR PROGRAMME ATTRIBUTES

PRODUCT/SERVICE/PROGRAMME 1

PRICE _____

FEATURES _____

_____

BENEFITS _____

POSITION RELATIVE TO SIMILAR PRODUCTS/SERVICES/PROGRAMMES IN PORTFOLIO

_____

_____

PRODUCT/SERVICE/PROGRAMME 2

PRICE _____

FEATURES _____

_____

BENEFITS _____

POSITION RELATIVE TO SIMILAR PRODUCTS/SERVICES/PROGRAMMES IN PORTFOLIO

_____

_____

and so on for each product/service/programme

Products/services/programmes to be promoted

This lists what the company is promoting. If there is a coding system, then the code should be entered. It may be used to tie budgetary requirements together. The customer database system will also need the codes, eg for lead handling and reporting. Where the product range being promoted is very broad, the codes for the main products should be entered. There may also be market sector or segment codes if the marketing is specialised along these lines. Geographic coding should be dealt with on Form 2 by adding an area code column.

Product or programme attributes

For each product or programme, one should specify the main details, as follows:

Price: The price the product is offered at. For programmes not involving the sale of a product, this will not apply, unless an entry price or subscription is charged.
Features: This applies to products and programmes. Main features only should be listed, eg a product's functions and performance parameters, the description of what the customer sees in a programme, eg a newsletter.
Benefits: How the product or programme will meet the objectives of target customers, expressed in customer language.
Position relative to similar products in portfolio: Where there are similar products, agencies need to know how to position this product relative to them.

The above data provides clues for the direct marketing agency in terms of claims that can be made and benefits which can be encapsulated into offers. It also provides a check on whether the targeting is correct.

List *all* the benefits the company wants to convey. Some media (such as television) work well conveying a single proposition very forcefully. This helps ensure that other campaign elements are noticed by customers. Some media, such as direct mail and other print elements, can handle several propositions and benefits simultaneously (though they should still be prioritised in some way).

FORM 5: MARKET DETAIL

CAMPAIGN NAME _____ CODE _____

ORIGINATOR _____ DATE OF ISSUE _____

TARGET MARKETS (customer types)

1. _____

2. _____

3. _____

4. _____

RELEVANT CUSTOMER PERCEPTIONS

_____

_____

DIRECT COMPETITION

COMPANY   PRODUCT   COMMENT (eg SW/OT VS YOUR OFFERING)

Target markets (customer types)

This states what sort of customers we are aiming the campaign at. Some may wish to adopt a coding or standard description system so that selection criteria for target markets can be more quickly matched to their system and accessed to identify past results. This data will be based on analysis of the marketing plan but will not necessarily describe the same target market. Here the target market is being stated for the promotion, not the entire marketing activity.

Relevant customer perceptions

What research tells us about customers, their feelings, perceptions, etc. Extracted from market research and perhaps responses to past campaigns.

Direct competition

This is vital for agencies as it tells them what they have to pitch their campaign against.

Companies

Main competitive companies for the specific product, in order of competitiveness.

Products

Names of their main products.

Comment

A brief comparison of the product with the company's offering (strengths, weaknesses, opportunities, threats) and will give the agency a clue about the main competitive angle to be taken. One is likely to need more space here, but a succinct summary never hurts (eg pricey but high quality, cheap and cheerful).

FORM 6: CAMPAIGN ELEMENTS

CAMPAIGN NAME _____ CODE _____

ORIGINATOR _____ DATE OF ISSUE _____

AT BRIEFING STAGE, ONLY COMPLETE Y/N COLUMN TO RECOMMEND TO
AGENCY BASED ON PAST EXPERIENCE WITH PRODUCT/MARKET OR TO
STATE MANDATORIES. WHEN FINAL CONCEPT AGREED, INSERT DETAILS

	Y/N	IMPLEMENTER	SUPPLIER CO.	SUPPLIER CONTACT	ELEM. CODE	BUDGET

PROCESSES
LIST SELECTION
LIST CLEANING
DATA CAPTURE
LIST RENTAL
TM I/B PRESS
CH I/B PRESS
TM I/B MAIL
CH I/B MAIL
TM I/B TV
TELEMART O/B
MAILING DESIGN
O/B POSTAGE
FULFIL POSTAGE
LIST FOR EVENT

NB. TM = telemarketing   I/B = inbound   O/B = outbound   CH = coupon handling

PRINT
BROCHURE
INSERT
LEAFLET
TAKE-ONE
LETTER
NEWSLETTER
MAGAZINE
FOLDER
CATALOGUE
ENVELOPES
HEADED PAPER

AD/MEDIA
SPECIALIST PRESS
GENERAL PRESS
RADIO
TV
FAX
ELECTRONIC

TOTAL

Form 6 lists all the direct marketing elements that will be required in the campaign. It should be completed by the campaign manager. This form is critical, as it lists all the detailed elements of the campaign. The term "element" refers to any deliverable, which may be a physical part of the campaign, such as a letter, or a service, such as deduplication.

In more complex campaigns, the exact tasks being carried out by each supplier may not be known by every supplier. This can cause problems. For example, if several media are used, with promotional material prepared by different agencies, and a variety of fulfilment packs sent, each prepared by different suppliers, the marketer may be the only one with an overview of all tasks. If something goes wrong and he or she is not there to deal with it, problems may be compounded because no-one knows who to warn.

The form will be filled in progressively as the details for the campaign become clear.

Implementer

This refers to the member of your staff who is responsible for the particular element.

Supplier company and supplier contact

In some cases, a supplier will be involved. The name of the supplying company and the contact within that company should also be entered.

Element code

Arguably, the marketer should have a system for coding each element in a campaign. If the process is computerised, this makes it easier to refer to particular tasks. This applies particularly if a computerised project management system is used, in which case each element would automatically be coded as a subproject. If a coding system is adopted, it also makes it easier to file and retrieve quotes.

Budget

This is set by the campaign manager. Marketers may not wish to break down costs to this level of detail. In our view, the more detailed the approach, the less vulnerable one will be to overcharging and the better one's control of costs will be. However, detail takes time. So the marketers may need to compromise between efficiency and delivery speed.

The deliverables listed on the left hand side are the normal ones for a direct marketing campaign. Note the specification of different kinds of telemarketing and coupon handling for different media.

FORM 7: INITIAL ESTIMATES

CAMPAIGN NAME _____ CODE _____

ORIGINATOR _____ DATE OF ISSUE _____

	ESTIMATED QUANTITY	ESTIMATED COST (£)
OUTBOUND MAILING	_____	_____
OUTBOUND TELEMARKETING	_____	_____
INBOUND COUPON RESPONSE	_____	_____
INBOUND TELEMARKETING	_____	_____
FULFILMENT	_____	_____
CONVERSION TO SALE	_____	_____
POSTAGE COSTS		_____
OTHER COSTS		_____
TOTAL COST		_____
TOTAL REVENUE		_____

This section provides a broad quantitative overview of the campaign. To complete these parts of the form it is necessary to have done the promotional budgeting. This section also informs suppliers of the key numbers in the campaign, so it serves as early warning of the company's demands on their services.

The form gives only the first estimates. Good practice suggests that as soon as the need for the campaign is identified, and at the latest after it is given the go ahead, likely costs should be estimated, using one's judgement on volume and contact strategies likely to be required. This is input into the final budgeting decision. When the budget is confirmed, agencies will be asked to quote via the brief. The budget previously set will give an indication of competitiveness of quotes. Where standard costs (eg per call handled, per mailing) are negotiated, the process will be simpler.

For the calculations needed to complete this form, use the response rate achieved in the relevant tests or examine similar campaigns (similar products, similar offers) run in similar target markets. A good rule of thumb to follow is to avoid spending most of the promotional budget on a mailing where there is no basis to predict the response rate. For example, allow 20% of contacts to be experimental, with 80% tried and tested, so the response rate is reasonably predictable.

Costings should be based on anticipated contact and response numbers (including fixed costs). Revenue per response should be gross revenue, as the method of measuring net revenues and contribution may vary. However, if there is an agreed measure, put it in and say so.

Estimated quantity

The volume involved.

Estimated cost

The total cost of each item (not the unit cost).

Outbound mailing

The initial mail pack (cost including design, print and handling by the mailing house, but excluding postage).

Outbound telemarketing

Telephone contact initiated by the marketer.

Inbound coupon response

Processing of coupons sent in by customers.

Inbound telemarketing

Handling calls coming in from customers.

Fulfilment

Subsequent mail packs (eg catalogues) — cost to include design, print and handling by the mailing house, but excluding postage.

Conversion to sale

Number of actual sales. If this is handled by the sales force, sales office or other branch staff, this should include the cost of the contact.

Postage costs

Total number of items (mail plus fulfilment) sent, and total postage cost.

Other costs

For example, fees of agencies not on a retainer, research.

Total costs

The total of the above elements. This should be compared to the planned objective, eg sales level, number of contacts.

FORM 8: MANAGEMENT AND MEDIA TIMING PLANS

CAMPAIGN NAME _____ CODE _____

ORIGINATOR _____ DATE OF ISSUE _____

BRIEFING/PLANNING	PLANNED DATE	ACTUAL DATE
Campaign confirmed		
Agency brief		
Proposition agreed		
Concept agreed		
Contact strategy agreed		
Media brief produced		
Confirm media plan		
Receive media details		
Issue media details to suppliers		
Systems team briefed by direct marketers		
Systems programme produced		
Internal lists ordered		
Lists produced		
External lists ordered		
External lists delivered		
Go/no go		
Check campaign logistics		
Brief internal staff (HQ/regions)		
Campaign live		
Campaign ends		
Evaluate results		
ADVERTISING		
Creative agreed		
Copy approved		
Artwork approved		
Copy dispatched		
Advertisements appear		

FORM 9: MAIL AND TELEMARKETING TIMING PLANS

CAMPAIGN NAME _____ CODE _____

ORIGINATOR _____ DATE OF ISSUE _____

MAIL	PLANNED DATE	ACTUAL DATE
Creative agreed		
Approve pack dummy		
Lists ordered		
Final copy approved		
Mailing/fulfilment houses briefed		
Print production schedule issued		
Approve artwork		
Artwork ready for print		
Laser proof approved		
Sign off live pack		
First mailing		
First fulfilment		

INBOUND TELEMARKETING		
Brief telemarketing agency/group		
Scripts agreed for testing		
Operator briefing		
Systems test		
Scripts revised after testing		
Scripts live		

OUTBOUND TELEMARKETING		
Brief telemarketing agency/group		
Scripts agreed for testing		
Operator briefing		
Systems test		
Scripts revised after testing		
Scripts live		

Forms 8 and 9 give planned and actual dates for each of five sets of tasks, from the overall management set (briefing and planning), to handling of direct marketing media (mail, inbound and outbound telemarketing and response advertising). Media milestones are built in to the briefing and planning set. Basic advertising milestones have been built in, although the advertising department will operate to its own more complex milestones.

The main aim of this form is to ensure that everyone involved in the campaign knows what they should be doing and when. Not all the steps may be needed, but one is likely to need to diary most of them in. Within each of the five groups of tasks, the items are more or less in chronological order, so even if it is not possible to plan all the dates, one should know that if one gets to a particular step and an earlier step has not been completed, something may be wrong.

Fill in the dates actually achieved. Keep all the campaign team up to date with actual achievements, as this will help them plan. If a deadline slips, it is better to tell everyone about it quickly, rather than waiting until it creates more problems later on.

The steps are drawn from a comprehensive task list (see Chapter 10). Marketers may find that they need to draw up a list more suited to their own requirements. Note that there are two different kinds of milestone: general milestones which apply to the whole project (eg go/no go, first mailing) and specific ones which apply to particular suppliers. A slip on general milestones is likely to have serious consequences for the whole project. A slip on specific supplier milestones may be recoverable (generally by spending more money).

Marketers may wish to manage their timing plan and campaign resources using project management software. If so, Chapter 9 shows how to do this.

FORM 10: FORMAL AGENCY QUOTE

CAMPAIGN NAME _____ CODE _____

ORIGINATOR _____ DATE OF ISSUE _____

ELEMENT OF CAMPAIGN _____ MEDIUM _____

SPECIFICATIONS _____

_____

£

COST BREAKDOWN _____ _____

_____ _____

_____ _____

_____ _____

_____ _____

_____ _____

TOTAL QUOTE   _____

and so on for each element of the campaign

The aim of this form is to formalise the quotation process, so that all elements of the campaign can be quoted for on a consistent basis. Many agencies are used to quoting an overall price, but we believe that good practice requires a breakdown of costs. Marketers may wish to mandate the type of cost breakdown for different elements. This form should be completed by each supplier for each element of the campaign, ie the supplier is the originator.

Element of campaign

This specifies which element of the campaign is being quoted for eg coupon handling.

Medium

This specifies whether it is for mail, telemarketing, press or TV advertising.

Specification

Brief description of element (eg coupon handling for campaign in question for advertisements in the national press during August 1990).

Cost breakdown

A cost breakdown, classified by agreement with the marketers (eg design, artwork, print).

Quote

The all-in cost for the element.

Delivery dates required for the quoted item must be included in the milestones in Form 9, and the contract with the supplier should refer to Form 9 (and the issue date of that form) in its terms and conditions. Any changes in deadlines should be recorded in a modification to the contract and in a change in Form 9.

FORM 11: OUTBOUND LIST SELECTION BRIEF

CAMPAIGN NAME _____ CODE _____

ORIGINATOR _____ DATE OF ISSUE _____

EXCLUSIONS

1. _____

2. _____

3. _____

4. _____

5. _____

6. _____

SPECIAL INSTRUCTIONS _____

DATA CONTENT _____ NO. OUTBOUND STREAMS _____

SELECTION 1

PRIORITY _____ TREATMENT CODE _____ EST QUANTITY _____

DESCRIPTION _____

CRITERIA _____

_____

_____

_____

_____

NATIONAL OR REGIONAL _____

SELECTION 2

PRIORITY _____ TREATMENT CODE _____ EST QUANTITY _____

DESCRIPTION _____

CRITERIA _____

_____

_____

_____

_____

NATIONAL OR REGIONAL _____

and so on for each selection

117

Form 11 instructs the database team how to identify which customers are going to receive particular treatments. The term "treatment" refers to the particular version of the campaign a customer segment will receive as their first contact, eg a mailing or a TV advertisement. It begins with:

Exclusions

A statement of those on the database to be excluded from all treatments in this campaign (eg known competitive customers, small businesses).

Special instructions

This will include any special instructions to the database team concerning how they are to go about selecting customers.

Data content

This states what data is asked for, eg title, name, address, telephone number, job title.

Number of outbound streams

The number of different outbound treatments being selected (eg those receiving different initial mailpacks or being contacted by the telemarketing agency with different scripts). This number tells the database team how many times the following section on the form will be filled in.

The rest of this form gives the details required to make each selection.

Priority

Where there is a possible overlap between selections for different treatments within the campaign. If so, we need to know in which treatment to put customers who belong to more than one group. (Thus customers in priorities 1 and 2 would be put into 1).

Treatment code

The campaign treatment code.

Estimated quantity

An estimate of the number of people that need to be contacted to achieve the campaign objective. If the number that satisfy the selection criteria is significantly different, then the database team know that they should call the marketers to see whether they want to change their criteria.

Description

A simple description of the type of customer being targeted for the treatment (eg one man businesses in the South of England).

Criteria

Specific selection criteria laid down by the marketers to select customers described in the description (eg all post codes in counties X, Y and Z).

National or regional

Whether the campaign is national or targeted at a specific region. The customer database will normally be organised with the company's own regional coding, which would be specified here.

FORM 12: INTERNAL LIST SELECTION BRIEF

CAMPAIGN NAME _____ CODE _____

ORIGINATOR _____ DATE OF ISSUE _____

List ID _____ Description _____

Selection from list _____

_____

Exclude _____

Database count _____ Approved _____

List ID _____ Description _____

Selection from list _____

_____

Exclude _____

Database count _____ Approved _____

List ID _____ Description _____

Selection from list _____

_____

Exclude _____

Database count _____ Approved _____

List ID _____ Description _____

Selection from list _____

_____

Exclude _____

Database count _____ Approved _____

List ID _____ Description _____

Selection from list _____

_____

Exclude _____

Database count _____ Approved _____

The database may be subdivided for marketing purposes into several lists, possibly overlapping. For example, the company may have a list of responders to previous promotions, a list of small customers, a list of known buyers of competitive products and so on. This situation is most likely if the database is relatively new. In this case, selecting whole lists or parts of those lists will be an efficient way of making the selection. This is because the characteristics of these lists are likely to be known.

In some cases, eg lists of top customers, approval to use them may be required. Such customers should be addressed as a separate selection, as one should be communicating with them in a different way (ie different mailing material).

List ID

The reference number of the list required.

Description

Description of the list.

Selection from list

The criteria for selecting from the list.

Exclude

Any exclusions from the selection.

Database count

The estimate of the number that the criteria will select. This may seem to put the cart before the horse, but if the list characteristics are well known, marketers should have some idea how many their selection will produce. This will tell the database team that they should contact the marketers if the selection produces a number very different from this. If they have direct access to the system, then this number will be the actual number selected by the criteria.

FORM 13: EXTERNAL LIST SELECTION BRIEF

CAMPAIGN NAME _____ CODE _____

ORIGINATOR _____ DATE OF ISSUE _____

Requirement _____

List identified _____

Broker _____ Estimated number _____ Planned receipt date _____

Requirement _____

List identified _____

Broker _____ Estimated number _____ Planned receipt date _____

Requirement _____

List identified _____

Broker _____ Estimated number _____ Planned receipt date _____

Requirement _____

List identified _____

Broker _____ Estimated number _____ Planned receipt date _____

Requirement _____

List identified _____

Broker _____ Estimated number _____ Planned receipt date _____

Requirement _____

List identified _____

Broker _____ Estimated number _____ Planned receipt date _____

Requirement _____

List identified _____

Broker _____ Estimated number _____ Planned receipt date _____

Where the lists are external, Form 13 can be used to communicate marketing plans to database administration for comment and, perhaps, suggestions as to better lists or whether the data might already be on the system.

Requirement

State here exactly what kind of customer one is trying to target. It is particularly important to be very specific about one's requirements. This section may be used to brief an agency and complete the rest of the information when the appropriate lists are determined. Note that it may be possible to reduce list costs if some customers matching the description can be found on the database.

List identifier

This is the name of the list.

Broker

The name of the broker supplying the list.

Estimated number

An estimate of the number of customers the marketer will be supplied with, or the number he or she has specified as the maximum.

Planned receipt date

The date by which the marketer has asked the list to be supplied.

FORM 14: CONTACT AND FULFILMENT STRATEGY

CAMPAIGN NAME _____ CODE _____

ORIGINATOR _____ DATE OF ISSUE _____

CAMPAIGN TELEPHONE NUMBER _____

MEDIA   START DATE   END DATE

1. _____ _____ _____

2. _____ _____ _____

3. _____ _____ _____

4. _____ _____ _____

LIST SOURCE _____ EST RESPONSE % _____

TREATMENT DESCRIPTIONS

1. _____

2. _____

3. _____

4. _____

5. _____

6. _____

7. _____

8. _____

9. _____

10. _____

PRODUCT OFFER LIST

1. _____

2. _____

3. _____

4. _____

5. _____

6. _____

7. _____

8. _____

9. _____

10. _____

Form 14 summarises some aspects of the strategy for contacting and responding to customers. It would be completed as a result of the agency's response to the brief and go as further briefing to all suppliers.

Campaign telephone number

The telephone number to be published for respondents to use. An increasing number of campaigns give customers the option of responding by telephone and mail. It is necessary to keep a clear record of which telephone numbers have been allocated to which campaign or the wrong numbers may be publicised for the campaign.

Media

Media to be used in contacting customers, and the planned start and end date of their use.

List source

This summarises whether the system or external lists are the source of the data, or both. Whatever the case, it should be recorded here, together with an estimated response, based on past experience with the list or type of selection.

Treatment descriptions

A short description of each treatment. As this is the agency's response, it may at first differ slightly from the treatments listed elsewhere. However, this form may be modified later as discussions proceed.

Product offer list

The description of the product or other offer to be given in each treatment listed above.

FORM 15: CONTACT AND FULFILMENT DETAILS

CAMPAIGN NAME _____ CODE _____

ORIGINATOR _____ DATE OF ISSUE _____

CONTACT STRATEGY

STEP ID _____ ACTION _____

TARGET SEGMENT _____

TIME INTERVAL _____ SEND LEADS TO _____

STEP ID _____ ACTION _____

TARGET SEGMENT _____

TIME INTERVAL _____ SEND LEADS TO _____

STEP ID _____ ACTION _____

TARGET SEGMENT _____

TIME INTERVAL _____ SEND LEADS TO _____

and so on for each step.

FULFILMENT

ITEM CODE PACK   REF NO. STEP ID NAME AND DESCRIPTION

_____ _____ _____ _____ _____

_____ _____ _____ _____ _____

_____ _____ _____ _____ _____

_____ _____ _____ _____ _____

Please note
This is main vehicle by which agency documents its response (not its quote). It is changed as you agree strategy, and becomes brief to systems team, so:
1. Diagrams to be attached, with each action coded, normally to be supplied by agency
2. Description of details may be cross-referenced to other sheets

Contact strategy

This lists the details of the contact strategy for each treatment. A separate head may be needed for each one of these sheets with the treatment code.

Step

Description of media step (eg mail, telemarket)

Action

What is done in the step, eg mail letter, mail brochure.

Time interval

How long after previous step the current step should be taken. This means that this space should be blank for the first step.

Send leads to

Where sales leads arise from a campaign, the destination of the leads should be specified, eg sales force, telesales office.

Fulfilment

This specifies which items are in which packs.

Item code

The code number for the item.

Pack

The pack it is to go into (eg mail responders' pack).

Ref no

The reference number of the pack.

Description

The description of the item.

FORM 16: CONTACT STRATEGY DIAGRAM

CAMPAIGN NAME .... CODE ....

ORIGINATOR .... DATE OF ISSUE ....

Segment name
Segment ID
Segment type
Step name
Media:
  Contact
  Response
Offer type
Pack ID
No. pieces
Pages

Segment name
Segment ID
Segment type
Step name
Media:
  Contact
  Response
Offer type
Pack ID
No. pieces
Pages

Form 16 summarises how to identify and contact target customers. In each box the following details should be entered:

Segment ID

The ID number of the selection, allocated by the system. If the company has no system for coding selections, it should. Each selection becomes in effect a list which has been used, and may be wanted again. At each stage of the campaign, different lists will be generated (initial target, responders, non-responders, etc). Unless there is a system for referring to them, the handling of the database could become cumbersome.

Segment type

This is a brief description of the segment.

Step name

The name of the step, eg initial contact, follow-up.

Media (Contact or response)

This states what media are being used for the contact and by what media the marketers expect to receive the response.

Offer type

This says what offer the company is making. It should have a system for classifying offers, eg membership, price discount, two for one. Do not forget that the offer is what makes the consumer want to respond — now!

Pack ID

The ID of the pack used.

No of pieces

The number of pieces in the pack.

Pages

The number of pages in the pack.
This diagram may look detailed but a good diagram (however large
the paper!) provides the clearest way of conveying the structure of
the campaign, particularly to mailing, telemarketing and fulfilment
houses.

FORM 17: DATA, FORMAT AND DELIVERY

CAMPAIGN NAME ⎯⎯⎯⎯⎯⎯⎯⎯⎯⎯ CODE ⎯⎯⎯⎯⎯⎯

ORIGINATOR ⎯⎯⎯⎯⎯⎯⎯⎯ DATE OF ISSUE ⎯⎯⎯⎯⎯⎯⎯

LIST USAGE (Y/N)

MAILING ⎯ TELEPHONE SCREENING ⎯ DATA ANALYSIS ⎯ DEDUPING ⎯

DATA DIVISION REQUIRED (e.g. subdivision of customers on separate tapes)

⎯⎯⎯⎯⎯⎯⎯⎯⎯⎯⎯⎯⎯⎯⎯⎯⎯⎯⎯⎯⎯⎯⎯⎯⎯⎯⎯⎯⎯⎯⎯

DATA CONTENT REQUIRED (Y/N) (e.g. screening criteria for output tapes)

Name ⎯⎯ Address ⎯⎯ Tel No. ⎯⎯ Job title ⎯⎯

Others ⎯⎯⎯⎯⎯⎯⎯⎯⎯⎯⎯⎯⎯⎯⎯⎯⎯⎯⎯⎯⎯⎯⎯⎯

⎯⎯⎯⎯⎯⎯⎯⎯⎯⎯⎯⎯⎯⎯⎯⎯⎯⎯⎯⎯⎯⎯⎯⎯⎯⎯⎯⎯⎯⎯⎯

LIST FORMAT REQUIRED

Mag tape ⎯⎯ Cartridge ⎯⎯

MAGNETIC TAPE FORMAT

Standard ⎯⎯ Other − specify ⎯⎯⎯⎯⎯⎯⎯⎯⎯⎯⎯⎯⎯⎯⎯

⎯⎯⎯⎯⎯⎯⎯⎯⎯⎯⎯⎯⎯⎯⎯⎯⎯⎯⎯⎯⎯⎯⎯⎯⎯⎯⎯⎯⎯⎯⎯

⎯⎯⎯⎯⎯⎯⎯⎯⎯⎯⎯⎯⎯⎯⎯⎯⎯⎯⎯⎯⎯⎯⎯⎯⎯⎯⎯⎯⎯⎯⎯

DATA DELIVERY ADDRESS ⎯⎯⎯⎯⎯⎯⎯⎯⎯⎯

⎯⎯⎯⎯⎯⎯⎯⎯⎯⎯

⎯⎯⎯⎯⎯⎯⎯⎯⎯⎯

MODE OF DELIVERY BIKE ⎯⎯ CAB ⎯⎯ POST ⎯⎯ OTHER⎯⎯⎯⎯⎯

DATE OF DELIVERY ⎯⎯⎯⎯⎯⎯⎯⎯⎯⎯

Form 17 specifies in more detail exactly how the data is to be made available from the system.

List usage

A multiple choice question, to indicate which of the following the list is to be used for: mailing, telephone screening, data analysis or deduping against another list. A list may be used for more than one purpose.

Data division required

This is not normally to be encouraged, as it is expensive. However, separate treatments might need to be on separate tapes, as they might be handled by different mailing houses.

Data content required

More detail on the exact content of the data. A standard list should be used here, to be supplemented by "specials".

List format required

Whether magnetic tape or cartridge is required.

Magnetic tape format

The company should have a standard format which it requires all its suppliers to use. However, there may be times when another format is required (eg if a mailing house the company is using for the first time cannot read the standard format).

Data delivery address

Where the data is to be delivered to.

Mode of delivery

How it is to be delivered.

Date of delivery

Self-explanatory.

FORM 18: REPORTS

CAMPAIGN NAME _____ CODE _____

ORIGINATOR _____ DATE OF ISSUE _____

STANDARD REPORTS

	REPORT NO.	FREQUENCY	SEND TO	DELIVERY MODE
1.				
2.				
3.				
4.				
5.				
6.				

SPECIAL REPORT FORMATS   TIMING

1.		
2.		
3.		
4.		
5.		

POST-CAMPAIGN REQUIREMENTS (e.g. analysis, lists of non-responders, archiving dates)

1.		
2.		
3.		
4.		
5.		

Form 18 enables marketers to ask the database team for standard and special reports.

Standard reports

Standard reports will normally be available from the system. This asks one to specify which ones are wanted, when they are required, to whom they are to be sent and how (eg bike, cab, post).

Special report formats

The precise format of each special report required.

Timing

Frequency of issue of special reports.

Post-campaign requirements

Any special reports needed after campaign close.

FORM 19: SYSTEMS FEEDBACK REPORT

CAMPAIGN NAME _____ CODE _____

ORIGINATOR _____ DATE OF ISSUE _____

TREATMENT   QUANTITY PULLED

_____   _____

_____   _____

_____   _____

_____   _____

_____   _____

_____   _____

_____   _____

COMPLETION DATE _____

DISPATCH DATE _____

COMMENTS (e.g. problems in interpreting brief or selecting data)

_____

_____

_____

After the database team has completed its programming/selection work, the marketers need to be briefed on the results. If they have direct access to the system, this form will not be needed.

Treatment

The ID and description of the treatment.

Quantity pulled

The number of customers satisfying the treatment selection criteria.

Completion data

The date on which the selection was made. This might be important where the number satisfying the selection criteria was changing quickly.

Dispatch date

When the data was sent.

Comments

Space for the database team to comment on the brief they received.

FORM 20: OUTBOUND TELEMARKETING

CAMPAIGN NAME ————————————— CODE ——————————

ORIGINATOR ————————————— DATE OF ISSUE ————————————

CALL TYPE (Y/N) NON-RESPONDER ⎯ LIST SCREEN ⎯ COLD ⎯

SALES TRACKING ⎯

OBJECTIVES

1. ———————————————————————————————

2. ———————————————————————————————

3. ———————————————————————————————

4. ———————————————————————————————

PRIME INFORMATION REQUIRED FROM RESPONDENT————————————

————————————————————————————————

QUERIES LIKELY TO ARISE DURING CALL

1. ———————————————————————————————

2. ———————————————————————————————

3. ———————————————————————————————

DETAILS TO BE GIVEN TO RESPONDENT (INCLUDING WHAT WILL HAPPEN
AFTER CALL)

1. ———————————————————————————————

2. ———————————————————————————————

3. ———————————————————————————————

HELP DESK INSTRUCTIONS ————————————————————

————————————————————————————————

————————————————————————————————

LIST SUPPLIED BY ————————————— CONTACT NAME ——————————

ADDRESS ————————————————————— TEL ————

QUANTITY ⎯⎯ VOLUME REQUIRED ⎯⎯ START DATE ⎯⎯ END DATE ⎯⎯

DATA TO BE RETURNED TO SYSTEM (Y/N) ——————————

IF NOT, GIVE INSTRUCTIONS————————————————————

REPORTING REQUIREMENTS

————————————————————————————————

————————————————————————————————

PLEASE SEND COPIES OF ALL TELEMARKETING SCRIPTS AT DRAFT AND
FINAL STAGE
PLEASE SEND CODING DETAILS FOR ANSWERS

Forms 20 and 21 form the main part of the brief to the telemarketing agency. If in-house telemarketing is used, it should still be briefed in this way.

Call type

The reason for making the call. These should be from a standard list (eg mail responder).

Objectives

The call objectives eg to check interest, commit to sales visit.

Prime information required

What we want to know.

Queries likely to arise during call

The sort of questions the respondent is likely to ask the caller.

Details to be given to the respondent

What the customer must be told.

Help desk instructions

What the help desk needs to know.

List supplied by

The company's system or an external one. The telemarketing agency needs a contact name and address in case there are any queries.

Quantity

The number of customers on the list.

Volume

The number of calls required.

Start and end date

Start and end date of calling — self-explanatory.

Data to be returned to the system

This will normally be yes, but may occasionally be no. If not, instructions are to be given.

Reporting requirements

Reports from the telemarketing agency required during and after the campaign.

FORM 21: ENQUIRY MANAGEMENT/ INBOUND TELEMARKETING

CAMPAIGN NAME _____ CODE _____

ORIGINATOR _____ DATE OF ISSUE _____

PLANNED SOURCE OF RESPONSE   PHONE NO.   COUPON (Y/N)

1. _____   _____   _____

2. _____   _____   _____

3. _____   _____   _____

OBJECTIVES OF ENQUIRY HANDLING

1. _____

2. _____

3. _____

PRIME INFORMATION REQUIRED FROM CALLER

_____

_____

QUERIES LIKELY TO ARISE DURING CALL

1. _____

2. _____

3. _____

DETAILS TO BE GIVEN TO CALLER (INCLUDING WHAT WILL HAPPEN AFTER CALL)

1. _____

2. _____

3. _____

COUPON REQUIREMENTS (address to be sent to, whether verification required)

_____

DATA TO BE RETURNED TO SYSTEM (Y/N) _____

IF NOT, WHERE DATA TO BE STORED _____

HELP DESK INSTRUCTIONS _____

_____

REPORTING REQUIREMENTS _____

_____

PLEASE SEND COPIES OF ALL TELEMARKETING SCRIPTS AT DRAFT AND FINAL STAGE
PLEASE SEND CODING DETAILS FOR ANSWERS

Planned source of response

Marketers specify here where the response will be coming to the telemarketing agency from (eg mailing, press insertion), the number publicised, and whether a coupon was offered as an option (so the agency knows whether there will be outbound calls to be made).

Objectives

The objectives of enquiry handling, eg to check the strength of interest, to commit to a sales visit.

Prime information required

What we want to know.

Queries likely to arise during call

The sort of questions the respondent is likely to ask the caller.

Details to be given to caller

What the customer must be told.

Coupon requirements

Where the customer is told to send the coupon to; what verification is required.

Data to be returned to system

This will normally be yes, but may occasionally be no. If not, instructions are to be given.

Help desk instructions

What the help desk needs to know.

Reporting requirements

Reports from the telemarketing agency required during and after the campaign.

FORM 22: QUESTIONNAIRE SUMMARY

CAMPAIGN NAME ———————————— CODE —————

ORIGINATOR ———————— DATE OF ISSUE —————————

ADDITIONAL QUESTIONS/ANSWERS ON TELEMARKETING SCRIPT

1. ——————————————————————————

2. ——————————————————————————

3. ——————————————————————————

4. ——————————————————————————

5. ——————————————————————————

MAIL QUESTIONNAIRE ID ——

QUESTION DESCRIPTION	ANSWER DESCRIPTION	QUEST. ID NO.	ANS. CODE

Form 22 summarises the questionnaires to be used in the campaign. As these may be of many different types, this form is placed here as a prompt that the questions to be asked must be set down clearly in order to brief all involved.

Supplementary questions/answers on the telemarketing script

There are many standard questions in telemarketing scripts which need not be covered here (eg identifiers). Here are listed the questions special to the campaign.

This form provides a convenient way of summarising a mail questionnaire. It will help to brief the house handling data entry for incoming questionnaires. The terms used on this form are as follows:

Question description: Short description of the question.
Answer description: Short description of the answer.
Question ID: The ID number for the question. Some questions might be asked in several different campaigns. A record of these questions should be requested, and each one given an ID number, so that the data can be collated across campaigns.
Answer code: The code which has been assigned to the respective answer.

The process for setting up a questionnaire is as follows:

(a) draft the questions to be asked
(b) identify relevant questions already asked in previous campaigns
(c) determine whether one can use these questions (and/or whether one can use some of the data already gathered)
(d) Finalise the questionnaire, in discussion with the agency
(e) Enter the questionnaire details on the form and into the database system. Then send it to the fulfilment house.

FORM 23: MEDIA — BROADCAST

CAMPAIGN NAME _____ CODE _____

ORIGINATOR _____ DATE OF ISSUE _____

MEDIA TYPE _____ TEL NO. _____

SUMMARY OF STRATEGY FOR MEDIUM AND TEST ELEMENTS_____

_____

TREATMENT CODE ____TITLE OF CREATIVE ____CHANNEL/STATION ____

TARGET AUDIENCE_____

TIMING PLAN (incl. coverage, frequency, time of day, position in programme)

_____

BUDGET _____

EVALUATION METHOD _____

TREATMENT CODE ____TITLE OF CREATIVE ____CHANNEL/STATION ____

TARGET AUDIENCE_____

TIMING PLAN (incl. coverage, frequency, time of day, position in programme)

_____

BUDGET _____

EVALUATION METHOD _____

TREATMENT CODE ____TITLE OF CREATIVE ____CHANNEL/STATION ____

TARGET AUDIENCE_____

TIMING PLAN (incl. coverage, frequency, time of day, position in programme)

_____

BUDGET _____

EVALUATION METHOD _____

and so on for each treatment

Forms 23 and 24 constitute the brief from marketer to the media people.

Media type

For example, radio, TV.

Telephone number

The telephone number to be publicised.

Summary of strategy

How (if at all) the medium is to be tested and what the role of the medium is.

Treatment code

Self-evident.

Title of creative

Agreed title of creative execution.

Channel station

Entered when the media plan comes through.

Target audience

Description of the required target audience.

Timing plan

Description of required coverage, timing and position, changed to actual when media plan comes through.

Budget

The media budget available, as planned by the marketers.

Evaluation method

To be specified by the marketers.

FORM 24: MEDIA — PRESS

CAMPAIGN NAME _____ CODE _____

ORIGINATOR _____ DATE OF ISSUE _____

MEDIA TYPE _____

SUMMARY OF STRATEGY FOR MEDIUM AND TEST ELEMENTS_____

_____

_____

NUMBER OF ADS _____

TREATMENT CODE _____ NAME _____ TITLE _____

TITLE OF CREATIVE _____ TEL NO _____

TARGET AUDIENCE_____

TARGET QUANTITY (CIRCULATION) _____

TIMING _____

_____

SIZE _____ COLOUR (y/n) _____ POSITION ON PAGE _____

POSITION IN PUBLICATION _____ COUPON RESPONSE (y/n) _____

EVALUATION METHOD _____

TREATMENT CODE _____ NAME _____ TITLE _____

TITLE OF CREATIVE _____ TEL NO _____

TARGET AUDIENCE_____

TARGET QUANTITY (CIRCULATION) _____

TIMING _____

_____

SIZE _____ COLOUR (y/n) _____ POSITION ON PAGE _____

POSITION IN PUBLICATION _____ COUPON RESPONSE (y/n) _____

EVALUATION METHOD _____

and so on for each treatment

As for Form 23, with the exception of the following.

Media type

For example, national, specialist, sector press.

Number of ads

Number of insertions to be made (outcome of media plan).

Treatment code

Code of treatment.

Name

Name of treatment.

Title

Title of publication.

Timing

Enter requirement first. Change to actual when media plan arrives.

Size

Size of advertisement.

Colour

Whether colour or black and white.

Position on page and in publication

Where ad is to be placed.

Coupon response

Whether a coupon is included.

FORM 25: FULFILMENT PACK SUMMARY

CAMPAIGN NAME _____ CODE _____

ORIGINATOR _____ DATE OF ISSUE _____

PACK CODE _____ DESCRIPTION _____

ITEM CODE _____ TITLE _____

QUANTITY _____ EST RESPONSE _____ MIN STOCK LEVEL _____

DUE DATE FOR DELIVERY _____

SUPPLIER _____

CONTACT NAME _____ TEL NO. _____

ITEM CODE _____ TITLE _____

QUANTITY _____ EST RESPONSE _____ MIN STOCK LEVEL _____

DUE DATE FOR DELIVERY _____

SUPPLIER _____

CONTACT NAME _____ TEL NO. _____

ITEM CODE _____ TITLE _____

QUANTITY _____ EST RESPONSE _____ MIN STOCK LEVEL _____

DUE DATE FOR DELIVERY _____

SUPPLIER _____

CONTACT NAME _____ TEL NO. _____

ITEM CODE _____ TITLE _____

QUANTITY _____ EST RESPONSE _____ MIN STOCK LEVEL _____

DUE DATE FOR DELIVERY _____

SUPPLIER _____

CONTACT NAME _____ TEL NO. _____

and so on for each item. Complete a new sheet for each pack.

Form 25 is part of the brief to the fulfilment house.

Pack code

As specified by the marketers.

Description of pack

For example, pack for responders to coupon.

Item code

Code of each item in pack.

Title

Title of each item in pack.

Quantity

Number required for campaign.

Estimated response

Expected number of respondents.

Min stock level

Minimum number of items to be held in stock at fulfilment house.

Due date for delivery

When the fulfilment house can expect to receive the item.

Supplier

Where the item is coming from.

Contact name and telephone number

Who and how to contact the supplier of the item.

FORM 26: FULFILMENT LETTER SUMMARY

CAMPAIGN NAME _____ CODE _____

ORIGINATOR _____ DATE OF ISSUE _____

PACK CODE _____ LETTER DESCRIPTION _____

_____

COPY SUPPLIER _____

CONTACT NAME _____ TEL NO. _____

LASERED _____ PRE-PRINTED _____ DROP-INS _____

SIGNATURE SUPPLIER _____

CONTACT NAME _____ TEL NO. _____

DIGITISED OR COLOUR _____

LETTERHEAD

REGION _____ HQ _____ PRODUCT GROUP _____ OTHER_____

SPECIAL INSTRUCTIONS

_____

_____

This form ensures that the fulfilment letter is prepared properly and matched to the right pack.

Pack code

Code of pack in which letter is to be inserted.

Letter description

Description of letter (eg letter to respondents requesting more information about product X).

Copy supplier

Company or department responsible for supplying copy.

Contact name and telephone number

Name and telephone number of person in that company or department.

Lasered, pre-printed or drop-ins

How the body of the letter is prepared.

Signature supplier

Company or department that supplies the signature.

Contact name and telephone number

Name and telephone number of person in that company or department.

Digitised or colour

Whether the signature is digitised for lasering or colour printed.

Letterhead

National or regional sales/marketing, customer service, product manager, etc.

Special instructions

Any further special instructions.

FORM 27: PRINT PRODUCTION AND DISTRIBUTION BRIEF

CAMPAIGN NAME _____ CODE _____

ORIGINATOR _____ DATE OF ISSUE _____

PACK CODE _____ ORDER QUANTITY _____

DATE OF ORDER _____ OUTBOUND MAILING OR FULFILMENT _____

PRINTER _____ DUE DATE OF DELIVERY _____ MIN STOCK LEVEL_____

STORE AT _____ COST _____

IS MATERIAL NEW OR REPLACEMENT? ___ PUBLICATION NO. REPLACE ___

DISPOSAL OF OLD STOCK (AND DATE) _____

PACK CODE _____ ORDER QUANTITY _____

DATE OF ORDER _____ OUTBOUND MAILING OR FULFILMENT _____

PRINTER _____ DUE DATE OF DELIVERY _____ MIN STOCK LEVEL_____

STORE AT _____ COST _____

IS MATERIAL NEW OR REPLACEMENT? ___ PUBLICATION NO. REPLACE ___

DISPOSAL OF OLD STOCK (AND DATE) _____

PACK CODE _____ ORDER QUANTITY _____

DATE OF ORDER _____ OUTBOUND MAILING OR FULFILMENT _____

PRINTER _____ DUE DATE OF DELIVERY _____ MIN STOCK LEVEL_____

STORE AT _____ COST _____

IS MATERIAL NEW OR REPLACEMENT? ___ PUBLICATION NO. REPLACE ___

DISPOSAL OF OLD STOCK (AND DATE) _____

and so on for each item

Form 27 briefs staff on warehousing and the helpline requirements. If the company is large we believe it is vital that it observes the agency practice of installing a helpline. Company staff will always be ringing up to ask for this or that piece of copy, to find out who is responsible for what, or to find out what stage a campaign is at.

Pack code

Code of pack.

Order quantity and date

Quantity of this order and its date.

Outbound mailing or fulfilment

Use of this item.

Printer

The company printing this item.

Due date of delivery

When the item is due in stock.

Minimum stock

Minimum stock to be held at distribution centre.

Store at

Location of storage.

Cost

Cost per item.

New or replacement

Whether material is new or replaces some other item.

Publication no. replaced

If a replacement item, reference numberr of item replaced.

Disposal of old stock

How and when the old stock is to be disposed of.

FORM 28: PRINT DELIVERY ADVICE

CAMPAIGN NAME _____ CODE _____

ORIGINATOR _____ DATE OF ISSUE _____

SPECIAL INSTRUCTIONS (eg collation)_____

PUBLICATION TITLE _____ REF _____

SAMPLE DELIVERY QUANTITY_____

SAMPLE   _____ DUE DATE _____
ADDRESS

QUANTITY	NO. PER PALLET	DELIVERY ADDRESS	CONTACT NAME	DUE DATE
_____	_____	_____	_____	_____
_____	_____	_____	_____	_____
_____	_____	_____	_____	_____
_____	_____	_____	_____	_____
_____	_____	_____	_____	_____
_____	_____	_____	_____	_____
_____	_____	_____	_____	_____

This tells the printer how to deliver and ensures that recipients are informed about what to expect.

Special instructions

Any special operations to be performed (eg collation, binding).

Publication title and ref

Title and reference number of publication.

Sample delivery quantity

Quantity to be delivered as a sample.

Sample address and due date

Delivery address and due date for sample.

The rest gives the delivery batches required, specified in terms of quantity in the batch, number on each pallet, delivery address for the batch, contact name or addressee for the batch, and the due date for delivery. This is required as different batches may go to different locations.

FORM 29: CAMPAIGN CLOSE REPORT

CAMPAIGN NAME ＿＿＿＿＿＿＿＿＿＿＿ CODE ＿＿＿＿＿＿

ORIGINATOR ＿＿＿＿＿＿＿＿＿ DATE OF ISSUE ＿＿＿＿＿＿＿

MAILING

TREAT ID	NUMBER SENT	UNIT COST	TOTAL COST	NO. OF ENQUIR	SALES ACT/BLE	NO. SLS F/BACK	LEADS RESULT	SALES RESULT	REVENUE RESULT
＿＿	＿＿	＿＿	＿＿	＿＿	＿＿	＿＿	＿＿	＿＿	＿＿
＿＿	＿＿	＿＿	＿＿	＿＿	＿＿	＿＿	＿＿	＿＿	＿＿
＿＿	＿＿	＿＿	＿＿	＿＿	＿＿	＿＿	＿＿	＿＿	＿＿
＿＿	＿＿	＿＿	＿＿	＿＿	＿＿	＿＿	＿＿	＿＿	＿＿
＿＿	＿＿	＿＿	＿＿	＿＿	＿＿	＿＿	＿＿	＿＿	＿＿

TELEMARKETING — INBOUND

TREAT ID	NO. OF ENQUIR	UNIT COST	TOTAL COST	PACKS SENT	SALES ACT/BLE	NO. SLS F/BACK	LEADS RESULT	SALES RESULT	REVENUE RESULT
＿＿	＿＿	＿＿	＿＿	＿＿	＿＿	＿＿	＿＿	＿＿	＿＿
＿＿	＿＿	＿＿	＿＿	＿＿	＿＿	＿＿	＿＿	＿＿	＿＿
＿＿	＿＿	＿＿	＿＿	＿＿	＿＿	＿＿	＿＿	＿＿	＿＿
＿＿	＿＿	＿＿	＿＿	＿＿	＿＿	＿＿	＿＿	＿＿	＿＿
＿＿	＿＿	＿＿	＿＿	＿＿	＿＿	＿＿	＿＿	＿＿	＿＿

TELEMARKETING — OUTBOUND

TREAT ID	NO. OF CALLS	UNIT COST	TOTAL COST	PACKS SENT	SALES ACT/BLE	NO. SLS F/BACK	LEADS RESULT	SALES RESULT	REVENUE RESULT
＿＿	＿＿	＿＿	＿＿	＿＿	＿＿	＿＿	＿＿	＿＿	＿＿
＿＿	＿＿	＿＿	＿＿	＿＿	＿＿	＿＿	＿＿	＿＿	＿＿
＿＿	＿＿	＿＿	＿＿	＿＿	＿＿	＿＿	＿＿	＿＿	＿＿
＿＿	＿＿	＿＿	＿＿	＿＿	＿＿	＿＿	＿＿	＿＿	＿＿
＿＿	＿＿	＿＿	＿＿	＿＿	＿＿	＿＿	＿＿	＿＿	＿＿

WHETHER OBJECTIVES MET ＿＿＿＿＿＿＿＿＿＿＿＿＿＿＿

LESSONS LEARNT ＿＿＿＿＿＿＿＿＿＿＿＿＿＿＿＿＿＿

＿＿＿＿＿＿＿＿＿＿＿＿＿＿＿＿＿＿＿＿＿＿＿＿＿＿

AMENDMENTS FOR ROLL-OUT ＿＿＿＿＿＿＿＿＿＿＿＿＿

＿＿＿＿＿＿＿＿＿＿＿＿＿＿＿＿＿＿＿＿＿＿＿＿＿＿

＿＿＿＿＿＿＿＿＿＿＿＿＿＿＿＿＿＿＿＿＿＿＿＿＿＿

All this information should be extracted from the customer database system. The three streams (mailing, outbound and inbound telemarketing) are almost identical. For each treatment, identified by its ID, the following data needs to be extracted:

(a) number sent (mailing), number of enquiries (inbound telemarketing), or number of calls (outbound telemarketing)
(b) unit cost of handling the customer
(c) total cost of contact strategy for this treatment
(d) number of enquiries made or packs sent
(e) how many of these enquiries were actionable by the sales staff
(f) how many of these enquiries sales staff actually fed back results on
(g) how many actual leads resulted
(h) how many sales were made
(i) what sales revenue was achieved.

Whether objectives met

Statement based on comparison of objectives and results.

Lessons learnt

What to do better next time and what to avoid, input by marketer at campaign close.

Amendments for roll-out

If this was a test, this is where to specify any changes required for roll-out.

This section shows how the master briefing forms might be completed for a home contents insurance campaign from a fictional company, Combined Insurance.

FORM 1: CAMPAIGN DEFINITION AND ACCOUNTABILITIES

CAMPAIGN NAME: Contents insurance for motor customers CODE: P22/90

ORIGINATOR: J. Smith, Product manager, Contents DATE OF ISSUE: 15/2/90

DESCRIPTION OF REQUIREMENT: Campaign to sell house contents insurance to existing motor policy holders

PLANNED LAUNCH DATE: 2/7/90 PLANNED CLOSE DATE: 20/8/90

MEASUREMENT CRITERIA: 1. Net profit
                        2. Proportion of customers selected actually buying

CAMPAIGN MANAGER:	Helen Jones Direct marketing manager	INTERNAL CLIENTS:	Colin Williams Marketing Director Peter Laurence Product manager, Motor

IMPLEMENTER'S NAME	IMPLEMENTER WORKLOAD
Helen Jones	15 DAYS BETWEEN 12/2/90 & 3/9/90
David Jenkins	20 DAYS BETWEEN 12/2/90 & 3/9/90
Marketing assistant	

SUPPLIERS

COMPANY	CONTACT NAME	OBJECTIVE/ROLE OF COMPANY ON CAMPAIGN
1. Mailmight	Oliver Pearson	Execute mailing and fulfilment
2. Insight DM	Chris Peters	Prepare mailing and fulfilment pieces
3. Teleforce	Ed Friend	Inbound telemarketing
4. M & K Co.	Joan Liscombe	Post-campaign research

OTHERS ON CIRCULATION LIST FOR ALL CAMPAIGN DOCUMENTATION (keep to minimum)

George Morris National Sales Manager

FORM 2: CAMPAIGN COVERAGE

CAMPAIGN NAME: Contents insurance for motor customers CODE: P22/90

ORIGINATOR: J. Smith, Product manager, Contents DATE OF ISSUE: 15/2/90

TEST OR ROLL OUT: Test

OBJECT OF TEST: Test creatives and selections

IF TEST, ROLL-OUT STRATEGY: Roll out successful creative nationally, using selections to optimise cost/coverage

REGION INVOLVEMENT
No selection by region

FORM 3: OBJECTIVES AND STRATEGY

CAMPAIGN NAME: Contents insurance for motor customers CODE: P22/90

ORIGINATOR: J. Smith, Product manager, Contents DATE OF ISSUE: 15/2/90

OBJECTIVES OF MARKETING STRATEGY OF WHICH CAMPAIGN FORMS PART
1. To increase average revenue per customer in existing customer base from £250 to £280
2. To increase profit per customer in existing customer base from £15 to £20

MAIN ELEMENTS OF OVERALL MARKETING STRATEGY
1. Launch of range of householder insurance products — contents, credit card, travel, etc.
2. Strong media presence to reinforce branding
3. First year incentives to customers taking up additional products

PROMOTIONAL OBJECTIVES
1. Gain 80% prompted awareness among motor customers that Combined Insurance offers additional insurance products
2. Achieve 10% of customer base requesting quotation
3. Achieve 3% of customer base taking up contents insurance within 6 months of campaign close.

REQUIRED CONSISTENCY WITH OTHER CAMPAIGNS AND ACTIVITIES
1. To be offered at time of motor insurance renewal
2. Avoid offering to customers with claims in process

DESIRED CUSTOMER RESPONSE
1. Apply for insurance

PROPOSITION
Take up Combined's contents insurance when you renew your motor insurance and you can save 20% of your first year's premium and 10% of your second year's premium.

PREVIOUS PROMOTIONAL ACTIVITY TARGETED AT THE SAME AUDIENCE:
Credit card insurance offer may have been mailed to some of customers selected.

FORM 4: PRODUCT OR PROGRAMME DETAIL

CAMPAIGN NAME: Contents insurance for motor customers CODE: P22/90

ORIGINATOR: J. Smith, Product manager, Contents DATE OF ISSUE: 15/2/90

PRODUCTS/SERVICES/PROGRAMMES TO BE PROMOTED/OFFERED   CODE
1. Home contents insurance   2230

PRODUCT OR PROGRAMME ATTRIBUTES

PRODUCT 1

PRICE: Range of 0.5–1.2% of amount insured, dependent on risk area.

FEATURES:
No claims bonus
Initial promotional discount
Fast track claims treatment
Option of automatic renewal with motor insurance
Rate of increase limited to inflation rate (subject to no claim)

BENEFITS: Keep yourself insured with the minimum of fuss and be sure that when you need to claim, your claim will be dealt with quickly and helpfully

POSITION RELATIVE TO SIMILAR PRODUCTS/SERVICES/PROGRAMMES IN PORTFOLIO
A natural extension of your relationship with Combined

FORM 5: MARKET DETAIL

CAMPAIGN NAME: Contents insurance for motor customers CODE: P22/90

ORIGINATOR: J. Smith, Product Manager, Contents DATE OF ISSUE: 15/2/90

TARGET MARKETS (customer types)
1. Customers with cars of Group 4 or above insurance class
2. Customers with 2 or more cars
3. Customers in "up-market" post code areas (Pinpoint coding attached)

RELEVANT CUSTOMER PERCEPTIONS
Customers don't see a natural link between motor and contents insurance. They expect contents insurance to be offered through different channels (e.g. part-time salesman, building society).

DIRECT COMPETITION

COMPANY	PRODUCT	COMMENT (e.g. SW/OT VS YOUR OFFERING)
General Insurance	Home Plan	Lower cost, no introductory discount, premia rise quicker
Helpful Insurance	House Protect	Higher cost, but offers larger initial discount
and several others		

Part 3:
Resources

Chapter 7

Managing Suppliers

In direct marketing, one may use several suppliers in each campaign, such as:

(a) fulfilment houses
(b) direct marketing agencies
(c) list suppliers and brokers
(d) computer bureaux
(e) print creative providers
(f) premium providers
(g) data providers
(h) telemarketing agencies
(i) print production

In preparing the campaign, it is necessary to work closely with them. However, they may also need to work with each other. If marketers expect to be working with a particular set of suppliers over several campaigns, they should bring them together at an early stage (and then at intervals during the period they are working together). They should get them to identify any management problems that have emerged and possible solutions. Many inter-supplier problems are caused by centralisation of communication. In practice, it is best if suppliers work closely with each other according to a tight brief from the marketers, the client. This is much better than their having to rely on the marketers being at the centre of a network of communication.

Selection of suppliers is an important first step. Obviously, there are many criteria by which one can select suppliers. They include:

(a) Creativity — do they provide that extra spark, but one which is consistent with the brief? For agencies, this may depend on the quality of the creative brief as well as on the quality of creative staff. Marketers should always sign off the creative brief themselves.

(b) Quality — is their work of a consistently high standard?

(c) Reliability — is it possible to rely on them to perform well every time?

(d) Ability to observe deadlines — do they meet all their deadlines? If there are problems, do they advise quickly enough, or try to hide them?

(e) Ability to understand marketers' needs

(f) Openness — are they honest?

(g) Ability to take criticism and bounce back with better solutions

(h) Price — do they give good value for money? This does not mean being cheap. Can they account properly for the money invested in them?

(i) Ability to work with others (marketers as client, and with other suppliers). Do they enter into the team spirit and not try to look good at others' expense? Do they accept problems as team problems?

(j) Ability to add value to marketers' efforts — do they execute the brief blindly or do they help achieve more by identifying weaknesses in the brief and remedying them?

Increasingly, large direct marketing users are putting the emphasis on *management quality* rather than creativity. Direct marketing relies greatly for its effectiveness on "managerial" factors. It is good management that translates the strategy of the campaign — targeting, timing, offer, creative and media — into action. In selecting a supplier, it is worth paying close attention to managerial factors such as:

(a) their management processes

(b) the management experience of staff

(c) budgetary and costing processes

(d) their clients' experiences (eg do they deliver on time, at the right quality, within budget).

Once a supplier is on board and working with marketers on campaigns, the following "good management" rules should be applied:

(a) Always give clear instructions. These should cover what is to be achieved, by when, by whom and at what cost. Use the forms in Chapter 6 as the basis for this.

(b) Explain the criteria by which each supplier will be judged — overall and on each job.

(c) Provide clear feedback according to these criteria.

(d) Reward good performance — by recognition.

(e) Punish bad performance, by querying or refusing invoices, or negotiating down fees. Eventually, ask for a repitch.

Controlling supplier costs

In theory, it should not be too difficult to control supplier costs. If one is well prepared, one should get proper quotations from each supplier. Competitive quotations should be compared and the best value for money (not the cheapest) should be selected. If marketers work within a limited number of agencies on a retainer basis, they should have the right to examine cost structures and benchmark them against other agencies. For work suppliers buy in, agency marketers should also establish clear benchmarks. This applies particularly to paper, printing, telephone calls and the other components of a direct marketing campaign.

In practice, of course, life is not so simple. There never seems to be the time to get the quotations in. Rarely does there seem to be the opportunity to validate an agency's costs or those of the suppliers they are using. The problem of cost control is endemic to marketing. Standards are sometimes difficult to determine. Few tasks are repeated. The pace of work seems to militate against a methodical approach to negotiating, measuring and controlling costs.

However, this is no excuse. If pressure of work is the problem, marketers should know that the money that can be saved by proper cost control of agency services will easily pay for the extra staff needed to manage the workload.

Cost overruns

One of the main problems is cost overruns. There are several reasons why overruns occur, often happening simultaneously. They are listed below, along with possible solutions.

1. Last-minute copy changes and missed approval deadlines

The alterations may be caused by changes in internal customers' requirements or stimulated by their inspection of final copy. Internal customers never seem to take the copy seriously until they see the final version. Where "final-copy-stimulated" revisions are a severe problem, they can be removed by using desk-top publishing techniques as an intermediate production stage. Producing something looking very like the final copy helps focus attention.

There may be lack of concern for the costs of changes. This is particularly likely if internal customers are not budget-accountable. If they are not, then it seems only sensible to make them accountable. Otherwise, the holder of budgetary authority should occasionally exercise the ultimate sanction of withdrawing a promotion if the costs overrun too much.

If they are budget-accountable, then the problem may be that they are simply unaware of the costs of late changes. In this situation the solution may be simply to make them aware of the costs of late changes early enough for them to avoid these changes.

2. Lack of criteria for judging supplier costs

In media buying and TV advertising production there are now more or less accepted ways of benchmarking costs. Such benchmarks are less strongly established for below the line areas such as direct marketing. If marketers run many direct marketing campaigns, they should have enough data on media, print and telemarketing costs to establish some benchmarks. Marketers may want to discuss this matter with users of direct marketing in other industries. They may even suggest initiating inter-company co-operation, similar to that achieved for television, to establish benchmarks. However, these benchmarks will only work if accompanied by proper reporting procedures, indicating where over- or under-benchmark is achieved and why.

3. Lack of negotiation with suppliers

Many direct marketing buyers do not see themselves as negotiators but rather as budget estimators and users. They often make estimates on the basis of a single quote. This is sometimes caused by time pressures — there is simply no time for competitive quotes. The first part of the solution to this is to train all buyers in negotiation and to ensure that management determines a negotiating strategy with each supplier. This includes situations of cost overrun, where additional billing should never be accepted without query and negotiation. The second part is to ensure that briefs are prepared earlier, to allow more time for negotiation.

4. Lack of feeling of cost-accountability

None of the above will work unless staff feel cost-accountable. Leadership on this should come from the direct marketing manager, who must implement a simple system of cost-reporting to indicate where problems lie. Success must be rewarded in appraisal, visibility and promotion. Ability to manage costs should be seen as an entry-gate to more senior management positions and a natural development of professionalism.

5. Lack of supplier cost-control

Many suppliers lack cost-control systems which account adequately for the expenditure of client money. If marketers have a good system for controlling costs, they should transfer it to their suppliers. Suppliers should be required to account for costs using the same criteria. This will help standardise procedures and ensure that the same base is being used for negotiation.

6. Lack of cost-control system

If marketers do not have a proper cost-control system, they will find it hard to control supplier costs. So, they should install one. The system should consist of:

(a) *Recording procedures*
This means having proper procedures for recording costs against cost centres.

(b) *Reporting procedures*
These include simple reports on performance relative to budget and benchmark, and reports on who is over- and under-running on budgets, with exception reports for severe cases.

(c) *Budgetary rules*
For example, no work without job number and budget cleared, no agreement without negotiation and reference to benchmarks, no change to specifications without cost implications being negotiated and agreed.

(d) *Benchmark processes*
For example, a database of costs, time-estimates and resulting charges from different suppliers for different kinds of task.

(e) *Management processes*
For example, clear and fast processes for determining and modifying budgets, so that suppliers are not encouraged to work ahead of budget because budget agreement is not finalised.

(f) *Management review*
For example, budgetary performance should become an important item in management meetings, in review of suppliers (a supplier whose budgets are consistently overrun is not being helpful) and in review of the relationship with internal customers. The issues that should be reviewed in this way include:

    (i) whether the supplier, in response to the brief, offers alternatives with significantly different costs and benefits

    (ii) whether suppliers stick to budgets

    (iii) whether communications budgeting is practised

    (iv) whether staff have the right resources and skills.

These points are considered below.

Offering alternatives within projects

Even if there is not enough time to get competitive quotes or if there is a strategic agreement with a single supplier, we believe that suppliers should always be asked to present alternatives. The briefing process should encourage suppliers to suggest different solutions. If the supplier believes that there is only one possible solution, the answer to this is that in most contracting situations options are asked for. Some requirements in a brief are not absolute but cost-dependent. With options, management can compare incremental costs and benefits. Even if the absolute value of a campaign is hard to judge, the relative values of different approaches can be judged. Marketers are not asking *whether* they should do the campaign but *how* they should do it.

One risk with options is that suppliers present "artificial" options as well as their preferred one. For example, they may present an option with little benefit at not much less cost and one with higher cost but little additional benefit. Briefing and management judgement should control this. Briefs should demand significantly different options with real benefits. Responses not offering good enough options should be referred back to the supplier. A second weapon to be used is competitive tendering within a circle of selected suppliers, so that the more good options a supplier offers, the better its chance of winning the contract.

Sticking to budgets

Most budgets are fixed on the basis of preliminary discussions with suppliers. The problem of sticking to budgets is therefore less acute than might be supposed. Instead, the problem may be escalating estimates prior to budget, or additional budgets being requested later. Where these occur, the problem may be lack of clarity on project scope. Here, new requirements are revealed in discussions or after project-initiation. The requirement here is for better briefing and better earlier visualisation and presentation of the scope and likely outturn of the campaign. This approach allows possible gaps and errors to be detected earlier. This applies, for example, to desktop publishing of copy.

A wider supplier/customer relationship issue lies behind this. This concerns who bears the risk. Suppliers may claim that requirements have changed. But this could be another way of saying that they made an incomplete diagnosis of client needs. Is the supplier accountable for identifying needs, checking scope and offering options so that all eventualities are covered? If needs identification is a separately contracted and budgeted stage, then the final contract is more likely to meet customer needs. This consultative approach should only be deployed where there is uncertainty about needs and where there are risks around outturns. These circumstances require more time and greater skills from marketers and their suppliers.

If delivery is not to specification, who bears the risk — the supplier or the customer? In much contracting, penalty arrangements are in force and often used on the cost of quality argument. If delivery is sub-standard (does not meet the customer requirement), then suppliers are asked not only to make good the work, but to pay rectification costs. At the moment few marketing suppliers apparently understand the idea of quality, its techniques and financial consequences. However, the time is ripe for such a move.

Communications budgeting

Basing budgets on marketing goals, required communication tasks and benchmarked task costs is generally thought to be the most professional approach. Doing this properly demands time and information; in this case information on the costs and outturns of past campaigns. If this information is well organised, then communications budgeting should not be too difficult. Researching and testing should support this approach.

Resources and skills

Implementing effective cost control requires resources (people, processes) and skills. Resources should be funded out of the costs saved. The skills issue is more complex. Some direct marketing staff find it hard (even impossible) to combine developing friendly, constructive relationships with suppliers with keeping a tight control over costs and negotiating hard. Some feel apologetic when querying costs and are happy to have the job done for them. This is unsatisfactory and requires dealing with.

This is because many suppliers have strategies to exploit their clients' weakness in this area. Thus, if payment is made on an item delivered basis, the strategy is to argue the case that a more complex delivery is "essential". This stance is particularly powerful when combined with a "no options are possible" declaration. Other strategies are to develop close relationships with individual client managers and to become involved in managing whole campaigns. In this situation, responsibility for deciding much of the "what" as well as the "how" falls to the supplier. Also, the full panoply of "hospitality and treating" techniques is deployed as only marketing service agencies know how!

Most direct marketing staff are aware of all this. In some companies, because of workloads, lack of a comprehensive approach for handling cost-effectiveness and lack of management attention, they have not resisted these tendencies. These supplier efforts are only part of professional account management. But the professional response is lacking — a firm supplier-management framework within which negotiation and supplier management skills are deployed. Both the framework and the skills are required — one cannot work without the other. Without the framework, individuals are exposed to the full pressure from suppliers. Without skills, the framework will be discovered by suppliers and manipulated to their ends.

Managing the strategic relationship with suppliers

Many client companies are moving towards an arrangement with suppliers whereby the latter receive an annually negotiated fee for their consultancy, account management, planning, and creative work. All other costs are charged at cost, with no mark-up and only when agreed.

In this situation, achievement of cost-effectiveness depends heavily on fee/mark-up negotiations and on close vetting of *content* of work, as competitive tendering is foregone or only weak.

Benchmarking methods can be used to improve the situation, particularly when using external experts with access to other sources of cost information. Competitive tendering can be introduced even within this framework. But using a restricted circle of suppliers for competitive tendering can lead to collusion and work-sharing by suppliers. Rationalising the number of suppliers helps achieve strategic coherence but can lead to this cosy circle emerging. On the other hand, repeated competitive tendering among suppliers may demoralise them. It is also very demanding of marketers and their time.

Here is our suggestion on how to handle this situation.

(a) Decide which areas the company wants to open to increased competition, whether on a period or campaign basis, whether on a complete or part-area basis. Previous justification for strategic commitment should be re-evaluated, as should arguments for a single supplier. This might lead to a distinction between core areas (where a single supplier is essential) and peripheral areas, where freer competition could prevail.

(b) Where strategic commitment is maintained, fee, cost and mark-up control should be enforced, but periodic tendering and negotiation should cover these elements up-front, on a competitive basis (eg every 2–3 years).

(c) For campaigns within relationships, a request-for-tender approach should be used. This would be part of the brief, but also ask for cost details and options. Supplier accountability for a consultative, quality, approach should be clear (ie accountability for output, not input).

(d) Relationship contracts should include the installation of quality and cost-control procedures (including progress reporting).

(e) Keep the supplier network reasonably wide. Separate between strategic large agencies, second tier agencies and fast-track agencies. It should be clear that favoured suppliers will need to pitch against others, who will be given some business to maintain interest. Marketers should sometimes (eg if a problem of shortage of suppliers has been identified) help develop smaller agencies so they can compete.

(f) The estimated and outturn costs of every campaign should be published as part of the cost control process, using standard formats (as used in the request for tender). Benchmarks should be developed from these and budget-setting should be based upon analysis of these costs.

Now for some more general rules (whether the supplier is strategic or not).

(a) The briefing process must give the supplier data needed for the development of options (eg relative priorities) and must ask specifically for options.

(b) The costs of each campaign should be subject to negotiation, even if within benchmarks (otherwise the benchmarks will beome a fixed price).

(c) Evaluate the costs and benefits of each option.

(d) Develop benchmarks for the most common delivery items. They should cover fixed costs (eg consultative work, design and development costs which are not option, size or scope dependent) and variable costs (one which are option, size or scope related, and production/delivery costs).

(e) If possible, the inputs (eg manpower and materials) which determine supplier costs should be measured. However, input cost management is more time-intensive and may lead to artificial constraints on supplier recommendations. However, understanding input costs *is* important in understanding output prices as charged to marketers. It is particularly important for setting benchmarks (how much time does it take to do X?) and assessing what output cost variations are appropriate for different options.

(f) Denominators/units of costs (both fixed and variable) should be agreed with agencies eg hour/day of consulting time, column inch or second of advertising, sq ft of exhibition stand, hour/day of training, page of letter/brochure or complete letter/brochure. The breakdown of units should, if possible, match job-reporting requirements. The argument that the units are not currently used by a supplier is irrelevant. The aim is to find a useful common denominator (between customer and supplier) for managing costs, from quotation through to implementation.

(g) Variations from contract should be assessed using these units. Thus, if the customer requires more, it should be specified using these units. If the supplier believes that the customer has changed the requirement, the cost of the change should be specified in terms of these units.

(h) Benchmarks should in general be published, although they may be withheld while undergoing development. If published, this should be as normal *maxima*, within which quotations should fall. They are the start, not the end of negotiation.

Conditions for exceptions may be published, though these should be tightly controlled and not adopted as a norm.

(i) Key ratios should also be published eg how much consulting/-concept development time per unit of delivery (eg per letter).

(j) If workloads do not permit a fully-benchmarked approach on every project, validation of quotes against benchmarks should be carried out randomly. Campaigns should be selected post-delivery, so that quotation and outturn can be evaluated.

(k) Negotiation should be based on proper training, preparation and support. If there is a financial expert in the marketing department, deploy him or her as trainer and support.

(l) Central records should be kept of all quotes and outturn costs in relation to them.

Negotiating with suppliers

The first step in good negotiation is to recognise that the situation *is* a negotiating situation. Negotiation implies compromise. If it is all give on one side, all take on the other, it is not a negotiation. This happens when bargaining power is unbalanced, when one side wants to do a deal much more than the other. If one is a buyer, one's ideal should be to avoid being on the weak end of this — by avoiding situations where it is *essential* to strike a deal with a particular supplier, and get on the strong end — where the supplier feels he or she *must* strike a deal with one. However, if the deal is really unbalanced, the supplier will aim to get out of the clinch, eg by developing other areas of business.

At the end of a good negotiation, both sides should feel they have won something. The outcome should be a balance, which both sides see as favourable to them. To achieve this golden situation, pre-negotiation preparation is required, as well as smart negotiation on the day.

Consider the different possible outcomes of a negotiation.

A wins, B loses; B will be more difficult to deal with next time and will be less committed to the settlement. A may become over-confident and this may complicate relationships with B.

A loses, B wins — as above, vice versa.

A loses, B loses — a compromise, with neither side achieving their main objectives and both more difficult to deal with and uncommitted.

A wins, B wins — the ideal, only possible if both trade, so they need to know what is tradable.

Preparation

This involves research, decisions and action. The research is to discover not only what the supplier requires. It is necessary to know how much he or she needs the business, what other business he or she has got or is developing, what his or her objectives are in selling to the company (and of course what one's own objectives are in buying from the supplier).

The research must cover the personal as well as the business situation — one is negotiating with an individual (or a team), not an institution. The people one is negotiating with need to do business with the company and to be seen to do so successfully (by their colleagues and peers). It is essential that marketers make sure they develop insight into suppliers' feelings and needs as well as the facts.

One must structure one's approach. Classify objectives into essential, desirable and nice to have. For certain variables (eg fees, markups), there may be a range, from the absolute maximum one is prepared to pay, to the absolute minimum the supplier is prepared to accept. Finding out the latter may be difficult or even impossible. But one may be able to do it by negotiating hard in a preliminary area, to get a good price, and then applying the precedent.

Avoid underestimating one's own strengths and overestimating those of the supplier. Remember the importance of the company's business to the supplier, and how much they are learning from the company. It is unnecessary (whatever they might say) to have one's ego boosted and be made to feel professional (a classic ploy). One should always remember who one works for!

The decisions required are mainly in the area of strategy. Marketers need to determine what (if any) long term role they want the supplier to play and how the contract in question fits into it. The company must have alternative suppliers available if marketers feel the negotiation is going to be really tough. If marketers are not confident of this, their negotiation will be weak.

The action required is a little bit like sparring. The aim is not only to convey to the supplier on what sort of basis one might want to work with him or her (eg costs, volume, etc). One also wants to create impressions in the supplier's mind about where one believes him or her to be strong and weak, the importance to him or her of doing business with the company and so on. One wants the supplier to believe that he or she needs the business and will benefit greatly from having it. One also wants the supplier to believe that it will open up significant further opportunities.

Negotiators should give suppliers due notice of the areas where they are going to be tough (eg on mark-ups). Springing nasty surprises at short notice is for courts of law where judgements are being made, not negotiations. They nearly always delay negotiations and may leave a bitter taste which colours subsequent relationships. In the end, remember, the negotiations are with a potential business partner, not an enemy.

Preparing packages

Negotiations with major suppliers usually require the development of a complex product/service/price package, considering it, changing it, developing new packages and so on. One way to do this is as follows:

Identify pay-offs

Identify the high pay-off or maximum benefit areas for the company and for the supplier. Note that these are not necessarily high volume areas. The high pay-off areas for the company may be areas where marketers believe that a small amount of expert input will solve major problems. Or they may be areas where marketers have a high volume of activity but have had difficulty in finding suppliers to do it cost-effectively.

On the supplier's side, volume considerations often dominate — they may apply fixed mark-up policies, so that volume and profit amount to the same thing. But they may be a little wiser and apply higher mark-ups to the use of really scarce resources (eg their most skilled people). Use questioning techniques to establish their pay-off areas, so that before going into a negotiation, one is able to draw up a list of what one believes their requirements are, prioritised by pay-off, and set it against one's own list. This will be invaluable later on.

Supplier's criteria

Identify the supplier's criteria for a successful deal and list them in order of priority. Once again, questioning is critical. The criteria will of course be closely related to pay-offs, but not necessarily in a simple manner. For example, the biggest pay-off area for the supplier may be in the supply of television commercial production. But its most important success criterion might be to persuade the company to let it produce TV commercials in new areas of activity.

Benefits and opportunities

Identify key benefits and opportunities. Here, one is trying to identify the different ways in which one can profitability use the services of the supplier. Although this might seem like doing the supplier's job for him or her, it is important to understand the full scope of his or her potential. For example, it may provide one with elements of a deal that can be offered to them to compensate for items one wants to take away, or for a reduced price.

Tradables

Identify tradable items, things which the company or the supplier want and which one believes can be traded. For example, one may want to trade concessions on costs for concessions on management processes (we will pay you a little more if you use it to put your house in order).

Alternatives

Develop several (at least two) alternative approaches to putting together the required deal. The development of options is a critical weapon in testing one's understanding of the situation. It also provides one with a very strong bargaining weapon. Include tradable items in the packages. Also, request at least two options from the supplier. This will test his or her understanding of one's requirements.

Costs and resources

Analyse the cost and resource implications of each option. Get the supplier to break down proposals into their individual elements, costed separately, and negotiate the elements separately.

Choose

Determine which option one favours and prepare arguments to justify it to the supplier.

Then begin the negotiation, at the right time!

Timing

Timing is critical. If one starts negotiations too late, one puts oneself under time pressure. One forces oneself to conclude a deal, possibly on unfavourable terms. So start the negotiations well in time, and start the preparation even earlier. If the negotiations can be timed so as to put the supplier under a little pressure, even better. Timing all *one's own* negotiations to take place over a short period, at the end or beginning of the business year, will put *oneself* under more pressure than them. If one is doing this, one should change to negotiating through the year. Take each supplier in turn. One will prepare better, be more relaxed and do better deals.

The negotiation proper

The negotiation is likely to start with a going-in position on both sides. This position is likely to be different, sometimes separated by quite a gulf. The two sides can usually be brought together by each side giving way on points which are of lower respective priority.

In bringing the sides closer together, one must give away one's tradables in the right order. Do not give away something that is valuable (eg a high mark-up on direct costs) before something which is less valuable (a small additional contract).

Keep the negotiations broad. Also, if the negotiation is focused on only one issue from the start, there can be little trading, only confrontation. If one is in the stronger position, one should succeed, but the supplier may eventually resign. One must be negotiating over a wide enough range of issues to be able to give as well as take.

It is essential to make sure that both parties who are negotiating are entitled to concede, accept and deliver concessions.

Try to identify in advance which concessions the supplier is most likely to ask for and analyse the costs in advance. It can be very powerful to concede something on the spot in order to gain a major concession from the supplier. But one may not feel happy about doing so unless one understands the implications of the concession. Also, one should try to steer the supplier to ask for the concessions that are the cheapest to the company.

Try to control the meeting. Set the agenda (but get the supplier's agreement to it) and pursue one's own logic, not the supplier's.

Negotiating style

Make it clear that there are other suppliers to go to, that every opportunity is being taken to evaluate relative performance. Let them know that what they are offering can be obtained elsewhere (perhaps not the whole package, but certainly elements of it). Do not make prior concessions, as these will be treated as a precedent and a new starting point to the negotiation, more favourable to the supplier.

If the supplier deploys the hard man/soft man technique, do not fall for it. If it is not possible to do the same, keep cool, note the concessions being requested, but treat the hard man and soft man as the same person and request consistency. If one has done one's preparation well (possibly role-playing it), one should have the confidence to avoid any psychological traps the supplier sets. But be nice to the supplier. Reward concessions with small concessions on one's own side, and build on agreements reached.

Do not hesitate to buy time to think. Ask for a break (even ten minutes can help) and ask to be left alone during it. If one needs another meeting, ask for it. Especially in complex negotiations, hold them on one's own territory, so one does not have to waste travel time. One will have less hesitation about breaking a meeting and asking for another. But during the negotiation period, one *must* schedule additional time for unforeseen meetings.

Do not tell the supplier more than he or she needs to know about one's own negotiating position. The more one tells, the more he or she will ask, because the more the supplier will know about what the company can afford. But do not let this destroy the attitude of trust so vital to partnership. Use the language of trust, warn the supplier to expect tough negotiation, but stay reassuring about the relationship.

Do not commit to a position that it is impossible to back down from. If one states impossible "must haves", it may kill negotiation.

But if one backs down from declared "must haves", the supplier will believe one will back down from anything.

Remember, one's perception of the state of the negotiation may be different from the supplier's, especially concerning what has been agreed. Test understanding often, by restating what one believes to have been agreed.

Do not start with a highly unrealistic demand (in one's own estimation). The supplier may claim one's demands to be unrealistic. But one should rely on one's own judgement, based upon thorough preparation, not the supplier's protestations. If it is hard to trade, use hypotheticals, eg "If we were to do this, what could you do?", or more directly, "Could you do that?". Then get the concession before conceding the point raised hypothetically.

If an objection is raised, find out whether it prevents one buying altogether. Do this by asking "Does this mean you don't want to supply to us?". Do not ever give "ball parks" — they will usually be taken as a starting point.

Personal behaviour

This is a difficult area, but critical. Here are a few rules:

(a) *Know the value of silence.* Do not interrupt, but listen and learn. Use time to think about the next step.

(b) Be positive, in manner, language and style.

(c) Be relaxed — do not make it seem too much hangs on the outcome. Over-anxiety leads to too many concessions.

(d) Do not talk down to, patronise, score points off or ridicule the supplier — it infuriates.

(e) If things get sticky, use questions and clarifications.

(f) Apply pressure when appropriate (time, money), but not all the time.

(g) If one feels one is being pushed too far, end the negotiation with dignity to give time to regroup and get advice.

(h) Use active listening skills (body language indicating receipt and understanding of messages, note taking).

(i) Listen to body language. Look for indications that compromise is imminent, and let it emerge or move it along with a bit of pressure.

In general, good negotiators:

(a)   use less irritator words
(b)   do not volunteer counter-proposals so quickly, as these are often seen as disagreements or rejections, particularly if they follow soon after a proposal
(c)   do less defending and attacking
(d)   label and explain their behaviour (except for disagreement) more (eg "What I'm doing here is to . . .")
(e)   ask more questions, do more testing of understanding feelings, and summarising, and give more commentaries on
(f)   use fewer reasons to support their position.

What makes a good negotiator?

In brief:

(a)   people whom both sides see as effective negotiators
(b)   people with long term track records of successful negotiation
(c)   people whose negotiated outcomes are successfully implemented.

Good negotiators do not spend more time planning — they plan better. They plan (and ask) more questions about the other side, rather than just planning their own actions. They consider a wider range of objectives, options and outcomes. They stress the common ground in their planning and their behaviour during negotiations. They take into account the longer term implications of the negotiation. But they do not impose a rigid sequence on events ("Let's settle X before we settle Y"). Instead, they take each issue as it comes.

Team style

If marketers are going in pairs or teams, they should decide roles and stick to them. Roles include leader, strategist, specialist support, summariser and recorder. These can be combined to good effect, eg the summariser asks clarificatory questions at sticky points. If there are problems, ask for a break.

Post-negotiation learning

Record what has been learnt from each negotiation. If there were failings, remedy them (eg by better planning, changing the team, training). Learn from successes too — what went right, why it went right, what elements of the negotiation can be repeated with other suppliers.

Finalising the contract

This covers how to:

(a) ensure detailed specification of the supplier's deliverables (or how to specify one's own deliverables)
(b) embody it in a contract.

Do not forget to summarise the detail of the agreement as well as the main headings; the detail is often the key to value for money. At worst, failure in this area may lead to legal action by either side.

The contract with the supplier should flow naturally out of the summarised conclusion to the negotiation. However, the problem with many negotiations is that, accidentally or deliberately, they fail to cover every aspect of the subsequent relationship that they should cover. This is discovered when the formal contract is being drawn up and may result in a return to negotiation.

There is only one answer to this — a persistent, almost dogmatic attention to detail, an insistence that the agreement be fully documented and that it be used as the basis for a contract.

The reader may ask whether nothing be taken on trust. Of course, it can. But when trust agreements go wrong, both sides may try to escape by claiming that the agreement was misrepresented in some way — "No, that's not what we agreed!" is what both sides agree to say. It is a nice way out and can be happily blamed on a misunderstanding. But not too often. Eventually, someone (involved in or close to the situation, and suffering from the stresses and perhaps the poor appraisals arising from failures, or more senior but suffering from the consequences of ill-defined agreements) wakes up to what is going on and decides to install a process to ensure that every agreement is:

(a) based on a clear understanding by both sides of the requirements of the situation, the resources required to deal with it, the resources actually available, likely problems, and so on

(b) clearly committed to by both sides

(c) properly documented, with deliverables, timing and resources clearly specified, in a form accessible to and agreed by both sides

(d) followed through professionally, so that whenever there is a risk of outcomes not meeting requirements, early warning signs stimulate corrective action

(e) reviewed afterwards, with any learning points identified and used to improve the relationship

(f) correctly positioned in relationship to other agreements (concurrent, past or future).

Obviously, the level of detail involved, agreed and contracted to varies with the type of project and the closeness of the relationship. A close working relationship does mean that certain things can be assumed. There may also be a framework agreement against which individual agreements are made.

What then, does a good "contract" specify? It specifies:

(a) What is to be delivered, at a level of detail agreed to be adequate to ensure that it can be managed and quality-controlled on both sides, including progress checks. This should cover the commitments of both sides, not just of the supplier.

(b) By whom it is to be delivered (individuals and teams, including contact names and when and how to access them).

(c) By when, overall and for particular stages.

(d) At what cost, overall and for individual elements of work (again, the level of detail depending on the type of work and the relationship).

(e) How delivery is to be measured, including types of review, milestones, etc.

(f) Whether payment is to be by inputs (time/resources) or outputs (results).

(g) Prices (of delivered units), fees (where an overall package has been agreed), or rates (where resources are being paid for on a unit basis).

(h) Terms of payment (invoicing, payment period, late payment, interest charges).

(i) Problem-handling (what to do if something goes wrong).

(j) How learning will be incorporated into the management of the relationship.

(k) Escape clauses — identifying likely reasons and consequences of using them.

Chapter 8

Managing Direct Marketing Through People

A company may be planning to start using direct marketing for the first time. It may have just started using it. Perhaps it aims to use it more widely or professionally. Whatever the situation, how well that company does in direct marketing depends critically on having the right people. This chapter shows how to ensure that people have the right skills and know how to use them. It also shows how to identify and deal with the many people problems to be faced in moving direct marketing forward.

Attitudes

This chapter is not just about skills. To make the people side work, it is necessary to consider how and why the company started to use direct marketing. It is necessary to take into account how it developed its approach to direct marketing over the years. A company's direct marketing history will partly determine the attitudes of staff and the skills they have. If the company uses direct marketing as the main element of its marketing mix, most marketers will understand how direct marketing works and will accept its disciplines.

But what if the company has only just started using direct marketing? What if it is slowly increasing its use of direct marketing, gradually integrating it into its portfolio of marketing approaches? In either case, there will be a much greater variety of attitudes towards direct marketing. Attitudes will also differ if direct marketing is seen as having a basically tactical role to play, as opposed to being the fundamental basis for some of the company's competitive strategies.

People's attitudes will also be affected by the state of development of direct marketing management processes. Initially, in most companies, these are quite rudimentary monitoring and control procedures. They are likely to be aimed at ensuring that each campaign yields some profit, sales or information. As a company gets more sophisticated in its use of direct marketing, it may develop project management systems for ensuring that campaigns hit the market on time. It may develop scheduling processes and systems, to ensure that campaigns do not overlap, and to ensure that markets are covered by the right campaigns. It may reorganise so as to deploy skills more effectively. The state of processes and procedures is critical. It dictates how fast marketers need to move to develop and organise the skills required for direct marketing.

Motivation

Another part of the background we need to consider is the motivation of individuals. Working in direct marketing is exciting and rewarding but there is a shortage of good staff. Keeping good staff is as difficult as in any area of marketing. This is not just a question of pay. Many do not leave for money (though some do!). They may leave because they are looking for a company where direct marketing is more accepted (where they will not have what they see as basic credibility battles to fight). They may leave because they find the company's particular application of direct marketing rather routine. They may want more challenge and excitement. They may be looking for more or less management responsibility, more or less opportunity to work with the experts.

Given these factors, this chapter devotes some space to the context in which direct marketing skills are developed and applied. This should enable marketers to adjust our recommendations to the particular situation of their company.

Skills

We start, however, with skills requirements. These are many. Very few marketing companies would claim that they had all the skills they required, in the quantities they require them. Developing and keeping the right mix and level of skills is a constant battle. The phrase "two steps forward, one step back" rings very true here. As soon as a company recruits and/or trains to the right levels, marketing needs may change or key staff may leave to join other companies. This section discusses the ideal mix of skills and what can be done to move towards the ideal, while recognising that the ideal will never be reached.

Management, personal and technical skills — an important distinction

In training, we usually distinguish between three fundamentally different types of skill, as follows:

(a) *Management skills* — the type of skill required to manage or work with teams of people in order to achieve a particular goal.
(b) *Personal skills* — the type of skill required for an individual to function well, as an individual, in a variety of contexts. These contexts include the family and friends, peers, subordinates and superiors at work. Many personal skills are important contributors to management skills.
(c) *Technical skills* — those relating to the individual's specialism. In direct marketing, these include direct marketing itself, statistical skills and computing skills.

The dividing line between these types of skill is not always neat. For example, in some areas a personal skill may also be a technical skill if it is an essential requirement for the job. The personal skills of self-presentation are also part of the technical skills of a major account salesperson, for example.

The distinction between these types of skill is very important. For example, when a company gets started in direct marketing, it tends to import technical skills (direct marketing, statistics, systems) because it is devoid of them. Its early training emphasis is on technical skills. As the company begins to take direct marketing more seriously and integrate it with its overall marketing approach, the size and significance of direct marketing projects grows. A much higher level of personal and management skills is required. The personal skills particularly needed include the ability to manage one's time, present concepts to others and influence and negotiate with them. The management skills required include the ability to implement complex direct marketing campaigns, using a mix of department staff, other members of the company and a variety of external suppliers. The task lists and checklists covered in Chapter 10 indicate the complexity of the tasks involved.

The jobs to be filled

The skills required can be better understood if we examine the jobs involved in direct marketing. There is no ideal direct marketing organisation. But there are a number of kinds of post which seem to occur in most direct marketing organisations. They are as follows:

The direct marketing manager

This person is the leader of the direct marketing organisation. He or she is likely to report either to a more general senior marketing manager (sometimes head of the marketing communications or marketing services organisation) or, more rarely, to a non-marketing person. In some organisations there is no direct marketing manager and direct marketing specialists are quite junior, reporting to marketing middle management. The highest level of seniority of specialist direct marketers is achieved in the largest companies and/or those with the most commitment to the discipline. The lowest level is achieved in smaller companies and/or those with least commitment. Where the direct marketing manager does exist, he or she is in a difficult position, particularly if he or she has a large number of staff. He or she may find it difficult to resist the temptation to get involved in detail instead of focusing on what he or she is paid to do — manage the direct marketing team.

The direct marketing specialist

This is the most frequently occurring direct marketing type. He or she is often recruited from an agency or another company for technical skills. Sometimes, however, he or she is taken from elsewhere in the organisation and thrown in at the deep end with a small injection of technical training. He or she is typically the one on whom the burden of developing campaigns and making them work devolves. It is these people who require the broadest mix of management and technical skills. Paradoxically, it is just these people who are often regarded as quite junior. They are under-invested in from a training perspective. Worst of all, they are not managed in a way which encourages them to develop the mix of skills they require.

The systems specialist

In smaller companies, much of the systems work is contracted to external suppliers. Here there are unlikely to be any systems specialists dedicated to direct marketing. However, in larger companies committed to their own customer marketing database, there may be many in-house systems specialists involved in direct marketing. They often arrive at this job from being assigned to it by the manager of their particular systems department. Some will be only temporarily involved, setting up and running-in the company's marketing system. Our experience is that such people need to develop additional areas of skill.

They need to develop a new technical area — direct marketing. But it also helps if they develop more general marketing skills. This is because they will increasingly be asked to help integrate the work of the direct marketers with the mainstream marketing approach of the company. This means, for example, drawing off customer data from more general marketing systems, and feeding back data gathered from direct marketing campaigns into marketing systems. It may mean devising decision support systems which can be used in all marketing contexts (eg management reporting systems).

In many cases, it is a company's involvement in the highly quantitative and systems-driven discipline of direct marketing that leads it to consider extending similar approaches to all marketing. The direct marketing systems specialist is then likely to be called upon to help. But if these specialists have never been developed in marketing beyond a basic understanding of direct marketing, they will be handicapped in their ability to contribute.

The statistician

In the early stages of the use of direct marketing, as with systems, most statistical expertise is hired in. This may be as part of a package deal with the direct marketing agency, which will undertake to carry out (or use specialist suppliers to carry out) the statistical analyses which are so central to direct marketing. However, at this stage, these analyses are likely to be relatively unsophisticated. They involve fairly simple comparisons between the results of different tests, different selections within a campaign and so on.

Then the company gets more sophisticated in its use of data, particularly if it develops its own customer marketing database. It begins to see the potential of using more advanced statistical techniques to analyse its customers and group them into categories likely to be more responsive to different kinds of offer. When this stage is reached, the strategic advantage gained from successful analyses of this kind make companies realise that they are dealing with a highly sensitive competitive issue. This makes them worried about using external suppliers. Also, the depth of the analysis required means that there are real gains in having internal experts. They know the company, its customers, its strategies and its data.

Good business statisticians are rare birds. They do not require great skills in statistical manipulation. This is done by sophisticated computer packages which can even tell them what is worth analysing.

A good direct marketing statistician must have insight and creativity but not be a statistical purist. Such a person must be prepared to live by the fundamental rule of direct marketing — what works, works. Most direct marketing statistics are "dirty statistics". These do not observe the nice theoretical rules of pure statistics, designed to provide scientific degrees of certainty in making predictions, rather than find by testing patterns which can be shown to continue (or not!). So, statisticians recruited into direct marketing for their technical skills must be trained in marketing and direct marketing. They must also be involved in some campaigns, so they can see the practical context in which their analyses are being put to use.

The wider organisation

Although the in-depth training requirement may be within the direct marketing department, most of those requiring training will be outside that department. They will be staff involved in marketing and sales who need to deploy direct marketing to achieve their objectives. These are the users or internal customers.

The workload may be allocated between the specialists and the users in many ways. At one extreme the users may do most of the work and the specialists may provide the infrastructure (eg the customer database, the agency roster, campaign scheduling approaches). In this case, users become "doers". At the other, the users may brief the specialists, who act on their behalf with all the suppliers. In this case, they are "internal customers". The reader's company may be at any position along this continuum.

Either way, users will need some training. Where users are "doers", they will need much of the training that a direct marketing specialist requires. Where users are "internal customers", they will need a limited amount of training. This should cover how direct marketing works, what it can do for them and what they need to do to ensure that the specialists can do a good job on their behalf (eg brief them well, give them clear deadlines and stick to their own side of the bargain).

Senior marketing management

Senior marketing management are important. They control the financial resources for recruiting staff, investing in systems and pay agencies. If the company has committed to direct marketing as a strategic move, which is going to make a big difference to its overall marketing approach, then senior management must receive training. They must receive enough for them to understand what they are taking on. If not, their understanding of direct marketing may be based on their experience in other companies, what they have read in the trade press, presentations on seminars and so forth. They may need to develop additional skills in managing marketing. Particular requirements here are likely to include:

(a) understanding direct marketing performance measures (eg campaign statistics — market measures and financial results);

(b) understanding how to relate resource allocation decisions to performance results;

(c) recruiting, motivating and appraising direct marketing staff;

(d) for companies developing internal customer databases, managing systems investment, and working closely with the information systems department.

This training is particularly likely to be needed if the company's marketing management has come from a different marketing culture. It may have come from the consumer brand culture, where marketing communications is driven strongly by sales promotion and media advertising. It may have come from technical product marketing, where marketing is driven strongly by product specification, sales management and after-sales support.

Key skill requirements in direct marketing

What then are the key skill requirements? In our view, they are these:

1. Fundamental marketing skills

The reader might be surprised by the number of people working in direct marketing whose level of knowledge of marketing and of certain direct marketing disciplines is weak. If they are direct marketing specialists who have been drawn from an agency (and before that were fresh graduates), they will have had little chance to develop broader marketing skills.

What kind of general marketing skills are required in direct marketing staff? Here is our shortlist:

(a) Customer-orientation: the ability to see things from the customer's point of view. In direct marketing, it is all too easy to get carried away with the technicalities of the approach. Direct marketers should be able to stand back from their work — a letter, a planned telephone call, a brochure or a catalogue — and see it as the target customer would see it. They should then be able to ask themselves, dispassionately, the question "What customer benefits are highlighted?" and be honest in answering. For example, they must be able to discern whether what is stated to be a benefit is actually a feature or an advantage. If they can, then they have the makings of good marketers!

(b) An understanding of different basic approaches to marketing — brand managed, sales force-driven, retailing and the like, how they work and why they work. This is an important part of the basic development of the direct marketer. This is because the work of a direct marketer often involves either supporting or substituting for one or other of these approaches. So the direct marketer must understand what they are and why they work.

(c) An understanding of the basic marketing approach. This covers identifying customers and their needs (conceptually and analytically) and determining ways to meet them profitably through the deployment of the marketing mix (product portfolio, price, promotion, distribution channels). This understanding is critical if the direct marketer is to be able to integrate the direct marketing approach with the company's approach.

(d) An understanding of the accepted approach to business and marketing planning. This relates to the early part of Chapter 2. It includes:

　　(i)　 environmental analysis (understanding what is going on in the company's business environment, from the detail of its chosen markets (eg how they can be segmented to understand more) to more general areas — the economy, technology, legal, social, etc)

　　(ii)　setting objectives based on the needs of "stakeholders" (shareholders, managers, workers, etc) and the constraints and opportunities offered by the business environment

　　(iii)　determining strategies based on these objectives

　　(iv)　creating ways to implement these strategies through specific policies

　　(v)　 implementation, monitoring and control, and feedback to objectives.

This is the kind of process which direct marketing will be integrating itself with. The direct marketer is often a very short-term planner by nature. But he or she must learn to create direct marketing strategies which make sense to those involved with the longer term planning horizons of the company. At the other end of the spectrum, the direct marketer must also devise ways of measuring results which match those applied to other areas of marketing.

Direct marketing skills

Many direct marketing specialists may have worked in an agency which specialised in one area of direct marketing (the most common is direct mail). If so, they may know little about other specialisms if none of the accounts on which they worked used them. Neglected specialisms may include telemarketing and catalogue marketing. A more serious lack may be in the area of campaign planning, where strong marketing disciplines need to be observed for the campaign to be robust and integrate well with the company's overall marketing strategy.

The kind of skills which we believe are needed, particularly by direct marketing specialists, but to some degree by most of those involved in direct marketing, are listed below. This list should be used in developing recruitment profiles as well as training requirements.

1. *Campaign planning*
This includes:
(a) Setting objectives for the campaign, derived from the marketing objectives for the market segment in question.
(b) Choice of product or service which should be promoted to the target market.
(c) Determination of how the product is going to be built into an offer (ie something designed to appeal strongly to target customers and to motivate them to buy now).
(d) Determination of timing of the campaign, taking into account factors such as customer buying cycles, product availability, the timing of other campaigns being mounted by the company or its competitors.
(e) Selection of individual customers for the promotion, using selection criteria based upon target market definition and the proven responsiveness of different customers to promotional

approaches through the media planned to be used. This may be through list rental or selections from the company's customer database.

(f) Media choice — choice of the right direct marketing medium for the target market and offer.

(g) Creative — determining how to express the offer through the chosen medium, usually proposed by the direct marketing agency and approved (often after revision) by the specialist.

2. *Direct mail*

This is the foremost direct marketing medium, where the specialist needs to understand such aspects as:

(a) What makes good copy — text, layout, graphics, etc, used to express the key features and benefits of the product, often following the idea of getting the customer to go through the attention, interest, desire and action cycle.

(b) Designing coupons to draw response.

(c) What subjects can be conveyed well in print.

(d) What mix of material can be successfully combined in one mailing.

(e) How to develop a relationship with customers over a series of mailings.

(f) Postal issues — postcoding, preferred sizes and weight limits.

(g) Print issues — what are the printing requirements of particularly mailpacks, where and how these requirements can be fulfilled.

(h) Catalogue design.

(i) Understanding the role of mailing and fulfilment houses and how to brief and manage them.

3. *Telemarketing*

This medium is of growing importance and brings with it its own set of skills requirements. These include:

(a) *Inbound telemarketing*
   (i) Planning the medium which solicits the call (typically press, television or mail).
   (ii) Ensuring that the customer is clearly directed to call the right number.
   (iii) Inbound script development.

(iv) Planning the resources for handling the calls (often contracted to outsiders).

(v) Ensuring that data systems are in place to log responses and the data arising from them.

(vi) Tracking these responses and ensuring that follow up actions (eg a mail pack or a sales call) take place.

(b) *Outbound telemarketing*

(i) Ensuring that the right data is available for the calls to be made (names, telephone numbers, data required during the call, scripts).

(ii) Outbound script development.

(iii) Target setting.

(iv) Understanding productivity and performance statistics.

Both kinds of telemarketing require a lot of man-management skills, in particular recruitment, motivation, team-building and team management, training and counselling.

4. *Use of other media for direct marketing*

If these are broadcast media, then the manager needs to understand how best to get hearers or viewers to pay attention to the medium, and then how to take action (often via a Freepost or 0800 number). If these are electronic media, such as Prestel or Teletext, then the key is to get the customer to page the appropriate number, which may require the placement of trailer advertisements on frequently consulted fact pages.

If these are published media, then placement of coupon, return address or 0800 number-bearing material must observe some basic rules of clarity and placement within the publication and on each page, while the limited space available (compared with a mailshot) requires a high degree of conciseness in expressing the benefits of the offer.

5. *Campaign management*

Once the campaign has been planned and the media for it chosen, the main task is to manage the campaign through to launch. This involves:

(a) Setting out the many tasks involved in preparing each element of the campaign.
(b) Determining the accountabilities.
(c) Determining the time required for each task and the sequencing.
(d) Allocating the tasks formally (including briefing all the external and internal parties involved).
(e) Monitoring the performance of these tasks to ensure that they are completed by their deadlines, rescheduling where overruns occur.
(f) Communicating to all involved parties the progress of the project.
(g) Ensuring that at the appropriate stages the right sign-offs are obtained.

6. *Project management*
This is a division of campaign management. We have already suggested that companies using direct marketing intensively would be well advised to invest in a paper-based or computerised project management system, formalising the process of campaign management. The direct marketing specialist then needs to observe the additional disciplines of the system, ie entering stages completed, using the system to recalculate deadlines if slips occur and so on.

7. *Supplier management*
This covers everything:

(a) Identifying suppliers who are capable of doing the job.
(b) Requesting the "pitch".
(c) Evaluating the pitch. Here, it is very important to strike a balance between creativity in copy and in marketing analysis on the one hand, and efficiency and organisation on the other. Given the shortage of management skills in many agencies, the thoroughness of an agency's management processes and the extent to which they are adhered to, are increasingly important.
(d) Supplier selection. Many larger users of direct marketing keep a roster of direct marketing agencies. Each has different capabilities. Some are good at the big creative cam-

paigns, others good at tactical "in-fills". Some are specialists in mail, others in telemarketing, and so on. Keeping a portfolio of suppliers and deploying them on different campaigns can be a very good strategy for keeping agencies in line. There is a risk of losing commitment and of the agency not developing an in-depth understanding of the marketing context for the product or market in question. The greater the variety of agencies, the more important are briefing skills. Where other kinds of supplier are concerned (eg fulfilment and mailing houses, telemarketing agencies, data analysis houses, etc) most of these points apply, except that the management process side is, if anything, even more important.

(e) Negotiation. The overhead costs of a campaign — setting it up, designing the copy, selecting prospects, etc, are usually a very high proportion of the total cost. This contrasts with media advertising, where media costs typically dominate all other costs. In this latter type of promotion, the negotiation is often done by specialist media buyers. But in direct marketing it is up to the direct marketing manager to negotiate prices with his or her many suppliers. In this, he or she may need the help of the purchasing department, but he or she should still have the basic purchasing and negotiation skills expected of anyone spending large sums.

(f) Contracting — specifying all the deliverables in detail and fixing fair commercial terms.

(g) Supplier control — monitoring the performance of the supplier, against the contract, identifying where it is lacking and applying influence or pressure to ensure that it is up to scratch.

8. *Personal skills*

The rather hectic nature of much direct marketing work means that personal disciplines are at a premium. In our experience, the most important ones (and the ones often conspicuous by their absence) are:

(a) communication — the amount of teamwork required to develop and launch direct marketing campaigns means that those involved need to be good communicators. This is not just for formal presentations, but also in the sense of keeping the team informed (staff and suppliers);

(b) teamworking skills (for the same reason that communication skills are required);

(c) time management and diarying. Direct marketing campaign development is characterised by deadline after deadline. To hit all the deadlines usually requires good diarying disciplines (to ensure that all deadlines are placed in the personal schedule) and good time management disciplines (to ensure that priorities are adhered to).

9. *Data and database skills*

Direct marketing is probably the most quantitative form of marketing. Direct marketers need to understand how customer databases are built and maintained. They must know what sort of data is required as the basis for successful promotions, how to analyse customer and promotional data to target campaigns and to determine which campaigns have proved most effective and so forth. They do not necessarily need to be able to carry out the analyses themselves, as these are often contracted out to third parties. But they must understand the basics of data analysis in order to make sense of the results. They also need to understand the structure of marketing databases and how the system in which they are housed affects how they can be used. If they are to be given on-line access to the company's marketing database, then they also need the skills to operate the system.

Is direct marketing significant to the company?

So far, we have identified the wide range of skills and abilities which are necessary in the direct marketing team. But before investing in developing or recruiting these skills, one must be sure that the investment is worth making. Remember, every single skill is available on a contract basis, including those of the direct marketing manager. Thus, in a small company, using direct marketing as a tactical support to other means of marketing, no specialisation is required. The marketing manager may hire in a specialist direct marketing consultant, working as a "hired hand", to co-ordinate everything. However, as use of direct marketing grows and it becomes more central to the company's marketing thinking, then some of these skills need to be brought in-house and incorporated into the main planning processes of the company.

If the company develops its own customer database, this too can be housed at a computer bureau, but as the database grows and is accessed with increasing frequency for campaign planning, selection or analytical purposes, the costs of holding it at a bureau are likely to be very high and may be prohibitive. Issues of data security may also arise.

At some stage, therefore, database skills will need to be brought in-house. With these may come the statistical skills, for if the company is using customer data so frequently, it should be deploying more advanced statistical techniques to ensure that it is using the data productively. The applier of these techniques must have an in-depth understanding of the company, its policies and its database to do his or her job properly, hence the need for this capability to be provided in-house.

So, as use of direct marketing grows, the number of staff requiring training in some or all of the skills will also grow. The depth of the training depends partly on whether users are doers or internal customers, as discussed earlier.

Are the same skills always required?

Although the broad management skills requirements are common across most industries, different types and sizes of companies need different mixes of direct marketing skills. The major differences are likely to be these:

Smaller companies

These are unlikely to be able to afford many or any dedicated direct marketing staff. Staff responsible for direct marketing activity will have as their main task the orchestration of external suppliers (often small companies themselves) to achieve effective campaigns at low cost. The skills of supplier management are likely to be at a premium (clear concise briefing, communication, monitoring and control, etc), as are the "efficient" personal skills, eg time management, diarying.

At the same time, the staff concerned will need to be closely involved with the development of overall marketing policy and probably be expected to contribute to it, rather than taking it as given. In such situations, the marketing all-rounder who is a personally effective worker is likely to be at a premium.

Larger companies

These can afford and do need specialists. Their tasks are likely to be more precisely allocated as part of an overall marketing plan. As specialists of various kinds, they will be "pitting their wits" against their opposite numbers in competitive companies, to gain an advantage over them. This degree of precision in job definition implies that these staff will be working as members of a large in-house team. The team needs to be communicated with, listened to and influenced, rather than told what to do. Even the external suppliers may not be appointed directly, but as part of a wider corporate, even international, policy. So in this case, the skills mix needs to be richer in the areas of team working, as well as there being depth in the particular specialism concerned.

Consumer marketers

Companies marketing mainly to consumers need to have skills relating to the more "mass-market" media — mail, inbound telemarketing, published and broadcast media, as these are likely to be used more intensively. They also need to understand the kinds of consumer data available from third parties and the kinds of analysis that can be carried out on such data to segment the market.

Business to business companies

These will need mass market skills if they are marketing to small businesses (whether as final or trade customers). However, if their market is mainly larger organisations, they will need specific strengths in the area of telemarketing (especially telephone account management) and using direct marketing in support of sales staff or large agents). In the latter case, they will need to be very strong in the skills of "working with". These include communicating, influencing, negotiation and functioning as part of a team. Sales forces are rightfully suspicious of new approaches to marketing which involve addressing people they see as "their" customers.

Long term relationship marketers

Companies marketing to customers who maintain a long term relationship with the company (or have potential for so doing), eg if the purchase is frequent, or if there are additional products and services which can be sold after the "main sale", require the skills of database marketing. This is because they will probably find the development of an in-house customer database cost-effective.

Operations-intense companies

Companies with "real" operations facilities (whether service or "hard" product, eg manufacturing, transport, product retailing) operate with more constraints in terms of their flexibility to customer needs (eg inventory, capacity) than companies without such facilities (eg personal or financial services). Although this distinction is not hard and fast, direct marketers in the former type of company need to plan further ahead and remain closely in touch with situations in inventory or capacity. There may be less flexibility in product design here. The latter type of company can often create products specifically for direct marketing campaigns. In the former type of company, direct marketers may need very good communications and influencing skills in order to work successfully with those responsible for product specification and delivery.

Company heritage

This is important. For example, a strong engineering heritage means that direct marketers will need to work closely with engineering-driven product management. They will need to educate them into the idea of marketing benefits rather than selling features and of designing products to fit markets rather than finding markets for pre-designed products.

A sales force-driven company will need to be educated away from thinking of direct marketing as just a lead-generating device, rather than as a way of managing markets. The idea of a sales person working to direct marketing disciplines will not be easily accepted. These disciplines include:

(a) total accountability for the cost-effectiveness of each call
(b) high visibility of this accountability
(c) measurement of sales force effectiveness against other potential media for contacting and doing business with customers
(d) structured calling programmes following clear contact strategies, often in combination with other media.

In this situation, the direct marketing manager may need to work on a long slow campaign to educate and motivate sales management.

Recruiting direct marketing staff

Once the company has developed a clear skills profile for the staff, it can also use this as a basis for recruitment. This applies to all categories of staff discussed above. In our view, much damage is done to direct marketing by lack of attention to the skills and personality requirements other than traditional direct marketing skills. The result of this is that many direct marketers end up in positions where they are real experts at targeting, media selection and judging creative input. But they are helpless when it comes to managing a complex network of relationships or project-managing a massive campaign.

Who really needs training?

As we mentioned above, the community requiring training in most companies is unlikely to consist just of specialists. Our experience is that there may be ten times as many specialists as non-specialists who need training. The first step is to use the company's plans to identify which areas of accountability are expected to be closely involved in direct marketing. They may be involved as:

(a) *Users*
These are actually responsible for putting together campaigns. They may be specialists (direct marketers) or general-

ists (marketers who have some other accountability but who have to do some direct marketing themselves).

(b) *Customers*

These ask or brief specialists to devise and implement campaigns to meet their needs.

(c) *Research*

This is a special category of users. They may be using data generated by or recruited for direct marketing to reach research conclusions for use in the wider marketing organisation.

(d) *Support*

These provide one or other of the various support functions required by users. They include specialists in print, systems, data analysis, systems support (ie those who help marketing staff to operate a company's direct marketing system). They also include database management (those who ensure that the company's customer database is of the quality and size required to meet the company's needs).

(e) *Senior marketing management*

Those who secure funding, create direction and manage resources.

The more closely someone is involved in determining the detail of each campaign, the more he or she will need training in the relevant skills. The more senior he or she is, the more he or she will need to be briefed about the skills, resources and workload involved in delivering direct marketing projects.

Auditing skills

Once one has determined requirements, how does one determine whether individuals meet those requirements? Here, we resort to the time-honoured tools of appraising staff skills: interviews, self-assessment forms, exercises and questionnaires.

Self-assessment

These are used to obtain staff's own views as to the skill areas that they feel need developing. For this feedback to be meaningful, staff must be clearly briefed on the kind of jobs they are likely to be asked to do. It is no use asking a brand manager who has never been involved in direct marketing which skills he or she feels he or she needs to develop if:

(a) that person has no idea what jobs he or she is likely to be asked to do
(b) he or she has no idea of the skills required to do those jobs.

The first step, therefore, before implementing self-assessment forms is to provide clear individual briefs to each member of staff. These may be written, but face-to-face briefs are best where the individual's likely career path is at issue. A self-assessment form then simply lists the topic and asks individuals to assess their current level of skills and their need to develop that skill area.

Exercises

These can use a whole range of techniques — written exercises, simulations, case studies, projects, role plays and so on. Role plays (often using case studies) provides a chance to assess the extent to which an individual works well in dealing with others, whether in the technical or the management area. Quite realistic simulations can be designed to run on computers, facing candidates with a series of decisions and assessing the consequences of them. Some companies have already built simple direct marketing simulations. These test the ability of the candidate to weigh up campaign response data and make decisions about the targeting of the next campaign based on their analysis of that response data. Written case studies and projects are used extensively in a variety of diploma courses (for marketing and other disciplines). The difference between the two is that the case study is about a given situation, the project about a situation that the candidate determines.

Questionnaires

Questionnaires can combine many elements of the above techniques. The questionnaire is singled out as a separate technique because it lends itself to computerisation and therefore rapid assessment and feedback. Once several batteries of questions have been written to deal with the different skill levels, they can be deployed flexibly to test the skill levels of individuals with different requirements. Computerised versions can also give very rapid summaries, recommending the main areas to be developed.

Questionnaires can cover anything from short questions to test direct marketing understanding (concepts, vocabulary, tactics), to more complex mini-case studies.

Interviews

The interview can serve one or both of two purposes:

(a) to enable the interviewer to establish more clearly the context in which the interviewee works, enabling the interviewer to customise course material properly
(b) to provide further information on skills requirements and, just as importantly, on attitudes towards the subject and the motivation to learn. Attitudes and motivation are strongly affected by how the interviewee is being managed currently.

The interview to establish training requirements is best covered when all the data from any other forms of assessment is available. The interviewer should familiarise himself or herself with this information before the interview and discuss the results with the interviewee. This is of course not an assessment for promotional purposes, but for training purposes, and this should be made clear (interviewees can be very suspicious, however careful one is to stress the purpose of the interview).

A summary of diagnostic interviews can be very helpful for management, provided that individual's names are not revealed. This summary may reveal to them how people feel about being introduced to a new discipline and what their concerns are. If a new marketing approach is being introduced, it is very common for management to feel that they have communicated the essence and requirements of the new approach very well. However, the recipients of the communication may feel that they are communicated with infrequently and incompletely.

When the data has been gathered, the training programme can be planned using data on the numbers requiring training and the type, breadth and depth of skills they require. This is a topic for specialist trainers and therefore outside the scope of this book. However, here are a few key points based on our training experience:

(a) Match the degree of involvement and the type of skills.

(b) Do not train too far in advance of the trainee's need to use the new skills.

(c) Do not overtrain — a small dose of training, followed by a large dose of experience, and then a further dose of training, is best. People learn by application.

(d) Get external input, even if the company uses in-house tutors entirely. Externals give trainees reference points and examples from other companies and build trainees' confidence that they are being trained to do something which is generally accepted practice. In other words, they are reassured that are not guinea pigs!

(e) Try to arrange for on-line use of the company's database. There is nothing like a realistic dose of data-entry to make trainees realise what is involved in setting up and analysing campaigns. But use a test database or otherwise it will create havoc!

(f) Use external courses to train in general principles, in-house courses for applying them to the company.

(g) Support trainees after the course — do not leave them in the wilderness. Follow the direct marketing principle of managing the dialogue with trainees after the "sale", to identify where they need additional skills and support.

After the investment?

If the company spends good money on recruiting and training good marketing staff, do not forget that this is only the beginning. Marketers must make sure that they follow all the principles of good management and work hard to keep their staff. Giving good training and user support will help. But here are some ideas as to how to keep staff in today's competitive labour market.

(a) Reward them for achievement. Build evaluation of their campaigns into their appraisal, and reward success by increased remuneration and promotion.

(b) Allow them to work towards success steadily, by giving staff small campaigns to work on initially, then build them to being able to handle large campaigns.

(c) Manage their workload. Direct marketing succeeds through management of detail. Do not expect staff to succeed if they are given very high workloads in some months and compensate for this by low workloads in others. Do not expect them to succeed either if they are continually given short notice of campaigns. They will find it very difficult to manage under these conditions.

(d) Allow them to contribute their expertise to strategy development. Accept and develop their ideas and give credit for them.

(e) Give them the opportunity to express their feelings about how they are being managed and what they are learning, through work and training. Use formal anonymous questionnaires and act on the findings.

Chapter 9

Systems and Statistics

In direct marketing, much of the emphasis has been on the kind of systems needed to hold the customer database (see, for example, *Database Marketing*, by Robert Shaw and Merlin Stone, Gower 1988). As the experience with these customer database systems grows, two important requirements are likely to emerge. These are for:

(a) management information systems to help manage the database and control campaigns
(b) a clear strategy for co-ordinating the development of the database and the direction campaigns take.

Management information systems

Big companies, running many campaigns on large customer databases, need management systems to achieve:

(a) development of a co-ordinated set of campaigns
(b) end-to-end management of each individual campaign, from conception to results.

The first part of this chapter identifies the requirements of these systems. However, it is not a detailed discussion of available marketing software. Nor is it a "how to do it" guide to systems design. This is not a book about marketing systems. The aim is to give some ideas about where to start in designing a direct marketing management system, and who to talk to.

The second part of this chapter picks out some systems and statistical questions that are likely to be faced as the approach to direct marketing evolves.

Where do we start?

Conventionally, there are two starting points for determining systems requirements. These are:

(a) what we have got today, and
(b) what we want tomorrow.

Theoretically, we should start with the latter and regard the former as a constraint. In practice, the problems of changing existing systems mean that what one has today is at least as important as what is wanted for tomorrow. Today's systems often determine the form in which one will implement tomorrow's requirements. So we start with a brief discussion of different kinds of system configuration and the constraints they are likely to impose.

The commonest kinds of configuration and their advantages and constraints are as follows.

(a) *Mainframe-held customer database, with campaign programming centralised*
Here, management statistics, such as volume of outbound contacts and responses, are usually reported directly by the mainframe system. There is no facility for project management, spreadsheet analysis and other management tools. Programming is carried out by an expert central team, which has a detailed knowledge of the main database software and of the contents of the database itself. This approach maximises the quality of campaign programming, but can increase the time required to plan a campaign. It gives little help to managers if they want to use the system to manage the campaign, and reporting is not always quick enough.

(b) *As above, but connected to management information systems*

Here, management statistics are usually extracted from the mainframe to various configurations of office systems. These might be microcomputers or minicomputers acting as file and communication servers to terminal networks. Project management, spreadsheet and other tools are deployed on campaign data through these systems. This approach provides high quality programming. It has the additional advantage that it provides campaign management facilities. However, there may be problems if the main database has to be redesigned. This kind of approach is also prone to data communications problems, particularly if users are widely distributed.

(c) *Mainframe-held database, with decentralised programming*
This may be achieved in two ways. Either the mainframe has been made easy for inexpert users to programme it, through a friendly (usually forms-driven) interface. Or the mainframe acts as a server to minicomputers or super-microcomputers on which all campaign programming and reporting is carried out. Programming and reporting is done by direct marketing or other marketing staff, not specialist systems staff. The latter provide professional support and validation. Tools as in 2 above are available. This system is technically most complex to set up but provides a high degree of flexibility while handling a very large customer database.

(d) *Minicomputer*
A minicomputer holds the customer database and all the tools required, programming and reporting as in (c) above. End-to-end campaign management is possible, but the database size is restricted.

The effect of the starting point

If the starting position is (c) or (d), then all that one has to do is to use the software provided to enter the details of campaigns, as per the forms in Chapter 6. If the starting position is (a) or (b), then some development work may be required by the systems staff to ensure that the management information system and customer database system are properly integrated.

The statistical tools required for analysing past response and other statistics to optimise future campaign targeting and offer development are deployed in various ways. On larger databases these tools are usually deployed on a sample file. This does not need to be updated frequently. However, the formulae derived from statistical analyses may occasionally have to be applied to spreadsheets for simulation purposes. Therefore, it is sensible to arrange some way of transferring data between the statistical sample file and planning spreadsheets.

What do we need?

To computerise the management of direct marketing, we need to computerise a number of areas in addition to the customer database. On the latter, we would expect to find records of customers, contacts with them and the campaigns that produce these contacts. The details held about each campaign are likely to be the following:

(a) target market, specified in terms of selection criteria
(b) product or service offer and associated revenue
(c) contact strategies, ie which actions (media and creative) are to be taken, with which customers, when, at what cost
(d) questions asked during the campaign and answers given
(e) measurement criteria and results.

The management information system needs to hold not only summaries of the above data, but also:

(a) details of the tasks required to get the campaign to market and the timings required
(b) intermediate policy data, which leads to the formulation of targeting and contact strategies (eg objectives, products positioning)
(c) technical data, for briefing the various suppliers involved (eg print and telemarketing requirements)
(d) data on people involved in producing the campaign (for electronic or physical mail addressing)
(e) simulation data, to show the effects of different approaches to targeting
(f) standard costings for different campaign elements, to allow quick estimation of costs
(g) actual costs.

As a campaign is developed, this data needs to be analysed, communicated, changed and reported. The communication is not only within the company, but also with a variety of suppliers. We believe that the minimum one should aim for is that the main suppliers be connected with the company on an electronic mail network. The best of all would be that they are able to log on directly to the management information system, with appropriate security.

Let us consider in more detail three particular pieces of software that one should have on the management information system, namely, database, project management and spreadsheet.

Database

This will be needed to keep all the details listed above. Through database software, all the facts of the campaign listed in Chapter 6 can be kept on file in a well-organised fashion. However, there may be longer pieces of text which cannot be reduced to a few words. It may be cumbersome to keep these using database software. In this case, simple word processing software will suffice, provided it is integrated with the database software. This will enable one to treat the name of the file where the text is stored as a piece of data and refer the user to it when appropriate.

Project management

This is needed to schedule the tasks required to deliver the campaign. Project management software asks one to input the lists of tasks required to produce the campaign. It asks what tasks precede others and by how much. It also asks what resources are needed for each task. It then recommends the best way of organising the tasks (timing, resource allocation). It also produces work schedules for the different resources involved. If there are delays, it allows one to reschedule.

Figures 9.1 and 9.2 show a simplified version of the output from such a programme. Figure 9.1 is what is called the Gantt Chart. It shows the tasks in the order one needs to start them in. It also shows:

(a) which tasks can be delayed without delaying the whole project, and for how long (free float)
(b) which tasks can be delayed and, while delaying another task, do not delay the whole project (float/delay)

	5 Days Per Symbol	02	06	10	17	21	26	30	04	08	13
ID	Task Name	Dec 89	Jan 90	Feb	Mar	Apr	May	Jun	Aug	Sep	Oct
001	Define market	X...
002	Campaign plan	XXXX ....
003	Produce brief	......X...
004	Agency response	......XXX ....
005	Agree strategy	..........XX ....
006	Confirm budget	...........X...
007	Go/no go	...........M...
008	Contact strategy	...............X...
010	Media plan	...............xx>>>>...
014	Determine lists	...............xx>>>>...
012	Creative work	...............XXXX ....
021	Plan fulfilment	...............xx ....
009	Do selections	...............xx ....
015	Order lists	.................xx ....
011	Order media	...................xxxxxxxxx > ....
013	Creative submit	...................X...
016	Creative agreed	...................M...
017	Copy/artwork	...................XXXX ....
018	Copy/art agreed	.......................M...
019	Pack finalised	.......................XX ....
020	Production begin	.........................M...
022	Printing	.........................XXXX ....
023	Lasering	...........................XX ....
024	Packs made up	...........................XXX ....
028	Ads appear	...............................m...
025	Mailing begins	...............................XX ....
026	Fulfilment	...............................XXXXXXXXXXXXXXXXXXX ....
027	Campaign close	....

xxx non crit	m milestone	>>> float/delay	XXX fin delay	=== unassigned
XXX crit	M crit milest	^^^free float	+++ crit fin delay	=== crit unass

Figure 9.1 Gantt Chart

(c)   which tasks which, if delayed, delay the whole project (crit).

Figure 9.2 shows the Pert Chart. This gives a graphical representation of the tasks and shows how they are connected to each other,
how long each takes and when each should be completed. It also
shows which tasks are on the critical path. Charts can also be produced showing loadings on individual resources (eg the agency) and
key dates for different people involved in the project. If one is running
many campaigns, the software allows resources to be scheduled over
them all.

Spreadsheet

This is much the simplest of all the tools, yet in many ways the
most powerful. It allows one to do complex repetitive calculations
involving many variables very simply. It is particularly useful for
costings. In our case, standard costs would be drawn from the database and placed into calculations to get estimated campaign costs.
The same model would be used for showing profitability, except this
time actual costs, revenues and response rates would be used. Figure
9.3 gives an example of calculations using different assumptions.
This would be based on test data. It gives the response rates and
conversion rates for the two different types of pack and the two
approaches to targeting. It shows that the best result is given by the
"Super" mailing pack, tightly targeted.

The spreadsheet should also be used for database modelling (Figure
9.4). This model is based on the idea that we recruit customers onto
the database using promotional campaigns. We then promote to them
to make profit. The target market is growing all the time. Therefore
the number of customers is also growing. So the calculations have
been simplified so that they can be presented on an annual basis.
The calculations for each promotion in a year are based on the
average size of the database in that year. This might lead to errors
in real life if promotional sizes and response rates were skewed
seasonally.

The final section of Figure 9.4, "Value of Customers on the Database", does not assume that this is a promotional benefit. It simply
shows the value of customers who are now on the database. The
implication is that knowing about these customers gives one a much
better chance of accessing them and defending their revenue.

Figure 9.2   Pert Chart

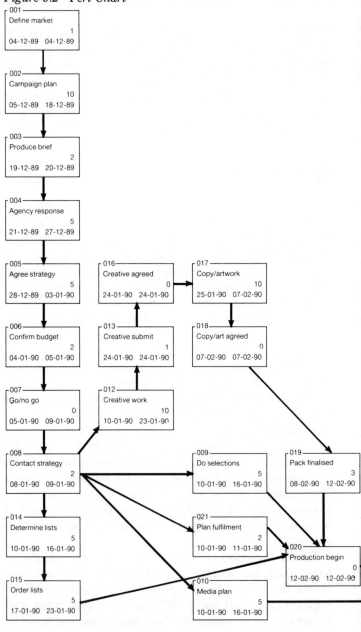

key

Task name	Duration (Days)
Start Date	End Date

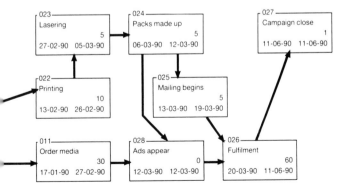

023
Lasering
                              5
27-02-90   05-03-90

024
Packs made up
                              5
06-03-90   12-03-90

027
Campaign close
                              1
11-06-90   11-06-90

022
Printing
                              10
13-02-90   26-02-90

025
Mailing begins
                              5
13-03-90   19-03-90

011
Order media
                              30
17-01-90   27-02-90

028
Ads appear
                              0
12-03-90   12-03-90

026
Fulfilment
                              60
20-03-90   11-06-90

		MASS MARKET		HIGHLY TARGETED	
1					
2	LETTER	Standard	Super	Standard	Super
3	Design	500.00	1000.00	500.00	1000.00
4	Unit print	.04	.10	.04	.10
5	Unit paper	.03	.05	.03	.05
6	Total cost	2600.00	5500.00	1200.00	2500.00
7					
8	ENVELOPE				
9	Design	300.00	400.00	300.00	400.00
10	Unit print	.02	.03	.02	.03
11	Base envelope cost	.03	.04	.03	.04
12	Total cost	1800.00	2500.00	800.00	1100.00
13					
14	LEAFLET				
15	Design	2000.00	3000.00	2000.00	3000.00
16	Unit print	.10	.15	.10	.15
17	Unit paper	.07	.10	.07	.10
18	Total cost	7100.00	10500.00	3700.00	5500.00
19					
20	POSTAGE				
21	Unit postage	.19	.23	.19	.23
22	Total postage	5700.00	6900.00	1900.00	2300.00
23					
24	Number mailed	30000.00	30000.00	10000.00	10000.00
25					
26	Total mailing cost	17200.00	25400.00	7600.00	11400.00
27					
28	COUPON RESPONSE				
29	Response rate	.04	.05	.07	.08
30	Number responding	1200.00	1500.00	700.00	800.00
31	Handling cost/coupon	.15	.15	.15	.15
32	Total handling cost	180.00	225.00	105.00	120.00
33	Outbound cost/call	5.00	5.00	5.00	5.00
34	Total outbound cost	6000.00	7500.00	3500.00	4000.00
35	Conversion rate	.07	.08	.10	.12
36	Number converted	84.00	120.00	70.00	96.00
37	Contribution/unit	150.00	150.00	150.00	150.00
38	Gross contribution	12600.00	18000.00	10500.00	14400.00
39	Net contribution	6420.00	10275.00	6895.00	10280.00
40	before mailing cost				
41					
42	TELEPHONE RESPONSE				
43	Response rate	.06	.07	.09	.10
44	Number responding	1800.00	2100.00	900.00	1000.00
45	Inbound cost/call	1.50	1.50	1.50	1.50
46	Total inbound cost	2700.00	3150.00	1350.00	1500.00
47	Conversion rate	.20	.22	.24	.26
48	Number converted	360.00	462.00	216.00	260.00
49	Contribution/unit	50.00	50.00	50.00	50.00
50	Gross contribution	18000.00	23100.00	10800.00	13000.00
51	Net contribution	15300.00	19950.00	9450.00	11500.00
52	before mailing cost				
53					
54	ALL RESPONSE MODES				
55	Net contribution	21720.00	30225.00	16345.00	21780.00
56	before mailing cost				
57	Net contribution	4520.00	4825.00	8745.00	10380.00
58	after mailing cost				

Figure 9.3 Spreadsheet analysis of campaign

		Year 1	Year 2	Year 3	Year 4
1	DATABASE MODEL				
2		Year 1	Year 2	Year 3	Year 4
3	CUSTOMER NUMBERS				
4	Start target market	1000000	1014670	1019632	1014646
5	Growth in target market	1.06	1.05	1.04	1.06
6	Gross target market	1060000	1065403	1060417	1075524
7	Less recruitment =				
8	End target market	1014670	1019632	1014646	1029530
9	Average target market	1007335	1017151	1017139	1022088
10	Number recruited	45330	45772	45771	45994
11	Proportion lost	.03	.03	.03	.03
12	Number lost	670	1996	3290	4549
13	Database total, year start	0	44660	88436	130916
14	Database total, year end	44660	88436	130916	172361
15	Average database total	22330	66548	109676	151639
16					
17	DATA/SYSTEMS COSTS				
18	Recruitment cost per head £	.5	.5	.5	.5
19	Total recruitment cost £k	23	23	23	23
20	Maintenance cost per head £	.4	.4	.4	.4
21	Total maintenance cost £k	9	27	44	61
22	Total systems cost £k	32	50	67	84
23					
24	RECRUITMENT CAMPAIGN DATA				
25	Proportion of target market				
26	promoted per promotion	1	1	1	1
27	Number promoted per promotion	1007335	1017151	1017139	1022088
28	Response rate	.05	.05	.05	.05
29	Number of responses per promotion	50367	50858	50857	51104
30	Conversion rate	.3	.3	.3	.3
31	Number recruited per promotion	15110	15257	15257	15331
32	Fixed cost per promotion £k	25	25	25	25
33	Variable cost per promotion £	.5	.5	.5	.5
34	Total cost of promotion £k	529	534	534	536
35	Variable cost per conversion £	.4	.4	.4	.4
36	Total cost per conversion £k	6	6	6	6
37	Total recruitment cost £k	535	540	540	542
38					
39	TOTAL IN ALL RECRUITMENT CAMPAIGNS				
40	Number of promotions	3	3	3	3
41	Total recruits	45330	45772	45771	45994
42	Total cost £k	1604	1619	1619	1627
43					
44	PRODUCT PROMOTION DATA				
45	Proportion of database	.5	.5	.5	.5
46	promoted per promotion				
47	Number promoted per promotion	11165	33274	54838	75819
48	Response rate	.15	.15	.15	.15
49	Number responses per promotion	1675	4991	8226	11373
50	Conversion rate	.3	.3	.3	.3
51	Number of sales per promotion	502	1497	2468	3412
52	Revenue per sale £k	.3	.3	.3	.3
53	Incremental revenue per promotion £k	151	449	740	1024
54	Profit margin	.15	.15	.15	.15
55	Contribution per promotion £k	23	67	111	154
56	Fixed cost per promotion £k	10	10	10	10
57	Variable cost £	.5	.5	.5	.5
58	Total cost of promotion £k	16	27	37	48
59	Net profit per promotion £k	7	41	74	106
60	Number of promotions	12	12	12	12
61	Total promotional profit £k	84	489	884	1267
62	Total systems cost £k	32	50	67	84
63	Total recruitment cost £k	535	540	540	542
64	Profit/loss £k	−482	−100	277	642
65					
66	VALUE OF CUSTOMERS ON DATABASE				
67	Sales per head	5	5	5	5
68	Total sales units	111650	332739	548380	758194
69	Revenue per sale £k	.3	.3	.3	.3
70	Total revenue £k	33495	99822	164514	227458
71	Profit margin £k	.15	.15	.15	.15
72	Total profit £k	5024	14973	24677	34119

Figure 9.4 Spreadsheet analysis of customer database

Computerising the campaign management forms

There are obvious benefits in computerising the campaign management forms presented in Chapter 6. Without this, running the process will be very cumbersome. There are two areas in particular that will benefit. Revising of forms will be much easier and issuing of reports will be facilitated.

As far as form revisions are concerned, it makes sense to keep a physical project file in which all revisions are stored. Going back to compare original and final objectives can make interesting reading! More seriously, the ability to track changes in campaign plans helps make accountability for campaign costs and results stick.

Without computerisation, reporting will be very slow and paper-intense. The kind of reports that will need to be issued include the following:

(a) projects at different statuses
(b) date each form was last updated
(c) milestones due and missed
(d) budgets allocated
(e) quotes accepted
(f) data missing
(g) results summary
(h) work loading on staff.

These reports can be run overall and for each direct marketing manager, internal customer, supplier, product and so on. Imagine the benefits of being able to show that a particular internal customer always briefed one late, or that a particular supplier was always late or consistently overran quotes!

Individual campaign reports should be filed with the campaign documentation. Many reports will be across-campaign and may be the subject for departmental review meetings.

To make it easy to keep a campaign running to schedule, it makes sense to develop standard memos. These should cover the campaign's transition between different statuses as per Chapter 5, chasing on milestones and cover notes for reports and form updates.

Developing the database in line with campaigns

Throughout this book, the assumption is that marketers are managing direct marketing in the context of a mature customer database. However, many companies, large and small, are at earlier stages of database development.

There are additional points that need to be watched if the company is at an early stage, and increasing the role of direct marketing in the marketing mix at the same time as it is developing its database.

Under these circumstances the work of the database marketing systems function or centre should be closely integrated with the marketing planning and implementation. Marketing policy, logistics and system capabilities must be developed together. Separating them organisationally risks one running ahead of the others. For example, too rapid an increase in the frequency and volume of mailing may strain the ability of the system to keep customer records updated.

Most companies which are now big users of long established customer databases would probably agree that one must have an agreed outline plan as to how the database marketing approach and its supporting system are to evolve. Without it, the centripetal forces that always exist in marketing and systems departments may lead to problems of lack of co-ordination and wasted resources. This plan does not need to be a rigid and very detailed action programme. But it must be based on an agreement as to the likely timing for implementation of the company's main direct marketing strategies. It should provide answers to the following questions.

Campaign development

(a) What kinds of campaign will be run in the future?
(b) Will they follow major general themes (eg customer loyalty, new product launches)?
(c) If so, what methodologies will be developed to maximise learning and effectiveness and minimise costs?
(d) What will be the balance between strategic communications and customer recruitment on the one hand and tactical promotions on the other?

These questions need answering because different kinds of campaign have different kinds of pay-off, use different kinds of data, and have different priorities. As users gain experience and confidence, campaigns will increase in sophistication. This will place a much greater load on marketing, statistical and systems services.

Testing

(a) *What testing strategies will be used in these campaigns?*
Promotion of new products and promotions to new customers require considerable testing of target segments and of contact strategies. Too much experimentation can lead to a waste of resources on statistical analysis before the fundamental characteristics and quality of the file are understood.

(b) *What are the testing priorities?*
There may be campaign priorities which lead to testing priorities which over-ride all others. For example, the need to increase customer loyalty or to recruit new customers may be paramount. If the first is so, then offer testing may dominate, if the second is so, testing of targeting may be most important.

Data strategy

(a) What will be the data acquisition and development strategy — overall and for different market segments?

(b) How will new sources of data be identified, qualified and tested?

(c) What is the long term questionnaire plan — frequency, breadth of market coverage, depth of questionnaire and what are its costs and benefits?

There are so many new data sources emerging that much of the data that would be needed for, say, the testing and subsequent launch of a new product may be available from external sources. If this is not so, a strategy for collecting relevant data must be developed. If mailed questionnaires are planned, the plan for obtaining, entering and testing the data must be properly defined and published. This will prevent acquisition of high volumes of information when low volumes would do.

Analysis strategy

Is a general segmentation programme to be developed?

Many companies are investing in tailor-made customer profiling. This provides them with convenient measures of customer characteristics and susceptibilities in relation to their own products and services. The benefit of these kinds of analysis is that they provide scorecards which can then be applied to any file with certain data elements. This reduces the volume of testing required and increases the response rates of campaigns. However, specific campaigns are usually required to bring in the data, and specific analysis programmes are needed to generate the requisite results.

Fine-targeted marketing

Will the company trial highly targeted marketing to assess areas of opportunity and deal with areas of threat?

In geographically-spread service businesses, locality marketing is being used more and more. This involves focusing on a tightly defined area, using direct marketing and a variety of geographically targetable media to obtain concentration, domination and repetition with great force. Such programmes can demand different ways of working (eg with sales forces, branch outlets and retailers). They may also require much deeper data to be gathered about customers in particular areas.

Media development strategy

Because direct marketing provides more accurate data on the effectiveness of different media, it can also show that *no* existing media are effective enough for accessing a particular market.

For larger companies, or companies with very deep penetration into particular markets, this can lead to the development of their own media (eg a customer newsletter or a catalogue) to access or maintain communication with a market.

New relationship development

How many new types of relationship will be launched?

Much successful long term direct marketing is based on the creation of special relationships with customers (credit cards, clubs, etc). Here, one of the major issues is how far "down" the "special affinity group" concept be used profitably. It is normally used to defend frequent users, but it can be used to defend and develop the less frequent user. In some cases, this is being done by adding new products and services to the relationship. Selling them can fund a frequency of communication with these users which cannot be justified on the basis of their purchases of the core product. However, this may mean that the database needs to be changed to include a large number of transient product categories.

New products and services

(a) What new products and services will be developed to add value to relationships? Who will be responsible for promoting and merchandising them? What value will they add to the company, eg profit, customer loyalty, funding of communication costs?

(b) Will these products include the sale of data to third parties or the use of the company's communications by third parties?

These may be a vital element in one's marketing plans. To ensure that these products and services are not seen by customers as attempts to exploit the relationship (eg bill stuffers), they should be carefully themed and developed. Products and services which might be supplied include not only merchandise, but information services, financial services and the like. These new products may require different types of data to be kept on the database.

Supplier development and management

What will be the role of different suppliers in developing new marketing concepts which can be implemented using the system?

We believe that it makes sense to involve agencies in marketing planning and campaign development. This is because, used properly, they can provide much insight into different ways of developing the customer relationship. One area where they may be needed is in developing combined advertising, sales promotion and direct marketing approaches to particular target markets. Some companies really test the mettle of direct marketing agencies by segmenting their market and allocating different segments to different agencies. They then compare the performance of the agencies with each other.

Joint ventures

Are joint ventures planned?

These may be with non-competing or partly competing suppliers, data providers and other marketing service companies, or major customers with an overlapping market. Where joint ventures are undertaken, data may be swopped and databases may be integrated.

Internal customers

How will all the above questions come to make sense to the different groups of internal customers? Will they become direct marketers themselves? What will be the consequences in terms of changes to the company's plans?

One may be able to put forward a fairly well-defined plan now. But it will almost certainly be changed by internal customers as they get their teeth into direct marketing! The plan will evolve, but always provide a basis against which change will be assessed.

Accountability

How will accountability for direct marketing be developed?

Internal customers have a responsibility for using marketing tools profitably. But they are also responsible for providing resources (eg data) and opportunities (eg developing promotional programmes which increase the value of the database). This ensures that these tools can continue to be used effectively. This responsibility is likely to "stick" better if internal customers are made accountable for it, just as sales forces in some companies are accountable not only for sales but also for the quality of the information they bring in.

Data acquisition and development issues

This section discusses some issues in:

(a) planning the acquisition, maintenance and use of new sets of customer data

   (b)   identifying statistical analyses likely to be effective.

Objectives

Data strategy is determined by business objectives, such as:

   (a)   generating customer loyalty (particularly through creation of affinity groups), sales (increased sales of existing products, identifying and capitalising on new product opportunities) and profit

   (b)   reducing marketing costs, eg through better targeting (lower promotional costs) or through using the database as a channel of distribution

   (c)   defending customers against competition

   (d)   adding value to the company's position in dealing with distributors or agents

How data help achieve these objectives

Customer data help achieve these by enabling us to identify more accurately:

   (a)   which of the company's products different types of people buy or do not buy

   (b)   what are the characteristics of buyers and non-buyers

   (c)   where we can find people of similar characteristics to buyers of particular products but who do not currently buy

   (d)   what appeals to them (whether in particular products or generally)

   (e)   what sort of promotion they are likely to respond to.

The process we recommend is as follows:

   (a)   Develop, using statistical analysis, detailed profiles of groups of "desired" individuals. The profile must contain some variables available on the database or on third party lists which cover the target markets.

(b)   Apply the profiles to the database or to third party data to generate a list of prospects for promotional programmes.

(c)   Promote to prospects an offer designed to appeal to the attitudes, interests and/or behaviour they are likely to have, supported by marketing campaigns through all channels.

We can apply this approach to *how* people buy (eg kind of channel) and to identify customers at competitive risk (eg by profiling frequent users of competitive products and identifying one's own customers with similar profiles).

As the database is built, efforts to develop better profiles (measured by the success of promotions using them) will improve a company's knowledge of its customers. Each campaign will be aimed at several segments, each based on a given profile. Productive segments should be reselected for later promotions, subject to controls on over-promotion. External sources of data should be judged on their contribution to the development of profiles which lead to better responses than profiles built without the external data.

The same methodology should be applied to the use of data-gathering questionnaires in the company's promotions. This can be used to ensure that the offers accompanying the main offer are appropriate to prospects' needs. Where these involve the sale of additional merchandise or services, we can obtain higher revenue from them, defraying some costs of the main promotion. Some offers may be from third parties, who "piggyback" on the company's mailings. They will be attracted by more accurate profiling. The data should also enable marketers to support, if required, branding and above the line advertising decisions.

Data maintenance

Credit card companies have monthly direct communication with customers. Few companies can afford this. But the more of one's customers one includes in affinity relationships, the less expensive updating will be.

One source of deterioration in consumer data is moving house. 10–20% of consumer customers may move each year. One might test mailing to incoming occupants, as the sociodemographic profile may be similar and they may be good prospects. Where a customer is not a member of an affinity group, one may fail to capture the new address, so one should keep using more accurately updated external lists that have pulled well before (deduplicated against the database). These may provide a way of recapturing movers (eg paid-for subscriptions to journals or associations) and regular mail order customers.

Apart from home movers, some categories of data date more quickly than others. Data maintenance strategy here depends upon:

(a) frequency of data change
(b) usefulness of the data to us
(c) ability to test ageing of data.

One way of testing the ageing of questionnaire data is questionnaire remailing to a sample of customers, asking them to answer the same questions they answered before. Comparisons are then run. This reveals how fast individual data items age. Marketers can continue to use older data with known inaccuracy if they cannot justify the cost of updating. If database capacity allows older data to be kept, we can produce tracks of change and use this as additional data.

The data maintenance strategy is therefore as follows:

(a) identify which items are of greatest use
(b) test via questionnaire remail to see which data have changed and how much
(c) calculate the data's decay rate, whether it is worth updating and how often
(d) mail repeat questionnaires (piggyback) covering data worth updating
(e) repeat the process at intervals determined by the ageing rate of the most useful data, including re-audit of information to identify the most useful elements.

Psychographic data from questionnaires

Psychographic questions relate to how people think or feel — a key determinant of buying behaviour. It is not easy to find out how people think or feel, so we focus on behaviour, the consequence of thought and feeling. Behaviour data is more plentiful and reliable. In direct marketing, we use buying data (frequency, recency, amount, category), together with data on consumer characteristics (household, income, etc). When we start direct marketing, we are looking for clues as to where to target activities because we are just building hard buying data. We may want to use three other main sets of data:

(a) respondents' reports of purchasing relevant products
(b) geosociodemographic data
(c) psychographic data.

The first two are good indicators of likely behaviour, although the second is usually overtaken by internal data. With psychographic data, responses to various attitudinal questions are used to build pictures of different types of consumer and then to segment the market. Thus, we may find that 15% of the population are "aspirers" (defined as those who respond in a certain way to certain questions) and design products for them. We do not have to identify individual aspirers if we are not using database marketing. We create an advertising campaign to appeal to them and ensure that it reaches groups of people thought to include high proportions of aspirers. With database marketing, we need more accurate identification of our target market. How then can we use psychographic responses via database marketing?

Take the example of the statement "Before I buy a holiday, I research prices to find the cheapest offer". Consumers agreeing with the statement are likely to be either more price sensitive *or* be more concerned about value for money (they want to be seen to be looking for the lowest price, even if they do not actually choose it). We can test what they mean by promoting to those who agreed and disagreed cheaper and more expensive holidays to the same destination, with different amounts of value added through extras.

If the statement is a good discriminator and if we have asked it on enough questionnaires, we can use it in other promotions as a selection criterion. If we are lucky, we might find that responses to the question tied closely to "harder" household data (eg a high proportion of self-employed C1 male consumers strongly agreed) and that this was also correlated with not taking up expensive offers. This would be very helpful in our targeting, provided that we insert the question in all our questionnaires. By experimenting, each company can build its own psychographic discriminators. These will very quickly outperform publicly available databases.

Aspirations data

This relates not to firm intentions, which are not always the best guide to future actions, but to "dreams", from the most prosaic (eg I would like to be able to afford to replace my windows) to the wildest (eg I want to retire early to California). If these are built into questionnaires, data reduction (see below) and profiling can be used to produce powerful psychographic segmentation.

Statistical analysis

Most early-stage database marketers find that very sophisticated statistical techniques are not required for post-promotional analysis and profiling. The main area where sophistication is needed is in data reduction. This involves taking a mass of data (eg purchasing, sociodemographic, psychographic) and finding out which data items best summarise the whole, eg if a customer lives in location X and answers "yes" to question W, then he or she is likely to answer Y to question Z and to buy product A. Automatic interaction detector techniques help here, as they give a good overview of the structure of the data.

The techniques likely to prove most useful once interaction has been detected are the standard ones of variance analysis and regression. Discriminant analysis has a long pedigree in product choice analysis. A variety of clustering techniques have been used to group consumers — this is the origin of much recent segmentation work. In any promotion, follow the principle that the selection/profile that pulled best should continue to be used until a better one can be found. However, multivariate analyses should be used to find out what distinguishes responders from non-reponders in a given cell, and cluster analysis to see whether there are any complex patterns of interdependence which account for the importance of discriminators.

Analyse responses by all possible segment dimensions (eg size, sector, degree of product usage in business markets; income, occupation, product usage, etc for consumer markets). Any clue as to whether the campaign was properly designed and targeted will help. Always segment by geographic area, as this may show handling differences, or differences in the success of a salesforce in closing. If the company has different contact and response vehicles, it may find that this is effectively a form of segmentation — telephone responders are different from mail responders. So, do not forget to analyse the characteristics of the two groups of responders.

Try to break down the response analyses in as fine detail as the market justifies. If the cells are too small, use multivariate techniques to establish the causes of variance in response. Remember that a very low response in a particular segment might mean that targeting was wrong or creative input was wrong. Research should show this.

Cluster-based segmentation involves finding groups of customers who share common characteristics. Questionnaires are often a good source of data for this. Clusters are a good basis for determining the creative element. They also provide a good way of filtering off different groups for different creative treatments at different stages of a campaign. One cannot rely solely on testing to arrive at the creative element. There must be something to test, based on one's knowledge of customers. Although the creative is often played down relative to targeting, targeted creative strategy is critical and not to be underrated. Once marketers have got it right, it seems unimportant as a cause of success, but it is an entry gate. Without a creative element written in the language of the cluster of consumers being addressed the response may be low.

If the company's campaigns are loyalty campaigns, marketers should not be depressed by poor early results. In our experience, loyalty campaigns take a lot of experimenting and learning to get right. Look carefully at the response figures for any clue as to why one group responded better than another. As loyalty campaigns lead the way to affinity groups, getting the language right is particularly important.

Next steps

So much for some of the areas marketers need to watch for as their approach to direct marketing develops. We hope that using proper planning and project management techniques, combined with professional analysis and a good deal of the right creative input, will get marketers where they want to go. Now, to help readers check that they have done it right, here are our checklists!

Chapter 10

Task Lists and Checklists

In this chapter, we have provided some task lists to help readers programme their project management system (or to write their management forms). We have also developed an extensive checklist. Its purpose is to help them ensure that they do not miss any actions and that they ensure that they get quality. Task lists cover the *what*. Checklists cover the *how*.

Task lists

Different campaign types may differ in terms of which tasks are required and in what order. Many tasks may run in parallel, so these lists are arranged by topic. A test campaign should involve the same tasks. If a campaign has already been tested, many stages may be omitted (eg creative/media work, market targeting).

Strategy

- Develop marketing plan
- Within marketing plan, determine market focus for campaign
- Identify customer needs in target market
- Select product or service for promotion

- Check customer database system for previous similar campaigns — type, product and customer coverage, level of success
- Confirm consistency with timing of other campaigns
- Trial selections run to confirm numbers in target market
- Determine budgets
- Set up outline campaign on database and management system
- Prepare draft timings (main milestones, not detailed project plan)
- Circulate draft timings to all suppliers and internal customers
- Receive supplier and internal customer comments and modify draft timings

Campaign management details

- Determine project management accountability — overall and in each supplier/department
- Prepare contact list and circulate to all suppliers
- Product and service details confirmed
- Campaign timing agreed
- Prepare draft agency brief using forms
- Issue draft brief to agency (or agencies if competitive tender being used)
- Agency comments on draft brief
- Brief finalised and confirmed
- Agency develops strategy, concepts, proposals and detailed timings
- Prepare detailed project plan in consultation with suppliers
- Prepare forms using checklist and based on marketing plan
- Review forms with management
- Agree forms
- Agency submits initial recommendation (creative, media etc.)
- Agency selected (if competitive pitch)
- Costs of recommendations evaluated against expected response
- Comment on recommendations, using checklists
- Agency revises recommendations
- Agency presents revised creative and media proposals
- Agency creative proposals agreed
- Agency media proposals agreed
- Campaign flowcharts prepared
- Campaign flowcharts circulated to all suppliers/departments

Pack preparation (applies to initial mailing and fulfilment packs)

- Prepare copy and layouts (letters, brochures, envelopes, etc)
- Prepare illustrations and photographs
- Review copy and layouts using checklists
- Revise copy and layouts if required
- Final copy approved
- Prepare artwork
- Check artwork, using checklists
- Revise artwork
- Approve artwork
- Prepare complete pack dummy
- Check pack dummy, using checklists
- Approve pack dummy
- Print sample run, for distribution to all involved in campaign
- Distribute samples
- Order all print for production runs

Internal communication

- Brief all sales and marketing staff
- Brief all other customer-facing staff
- Receive confirmation from customer-facing staff that briefs received, understood and agreed, and that mechanism exists for handling results of campaign (lead-handling, follow-up)
- Schedule training and motivation meetings if required
- Prepare training and motivational material
- Hold training and motivation meetings

General and system logistics

- Go/no go
- Campaign logistics checked with mailing, telemarketing, response handling and fulfilment agencies
- Check data links between all parties
- Agree selection/list
- Determine testing strategy (including test and control cells)
- Determine list size
- Select contact strategies

- Confirm selection rules and timing for initial target customer groups for each campaign action/treatment, allocate codes and enter into system
- Confirm rules for allocation to follow-up groups, allocate codes and enter into system
- Write custom selection routines if required
- Run trial extract/selection on test basis
- Check trial extract/selection
- Modify extract/selection programme if required
- Run extract/selection on production basis
- Check output file
- Transfer to desired medium
- Despatch output
- Check with recipient(s) that output correct/readable
- Go live
- Update promotion histories
- Receive updates from fulfilment/telemarketing agencies
- Update contact records
- Report production
- Campaign close
- Outstanding enquiries archived
- Final campaign report prepared and issued

Print and mail logistics

- Brief mailing and fulfilment houses using briefing format
- Print production schedule developed
- Print production schedule issued
- Prepare artwork for print
- Prepare laser letters with variations to match source and targeting and (for fulfilment letters) outcome of customer response
- Check sample letters using checklists
- Confirm outbound mailing envelope description
- Confirm fulfilment pack envelope description
- Define mailing and fulfilment packs on system
- Confirm media slots and timing
- Issue final media schedule
- Print outbound mailing
- Check samples of outbound mailing using checklists
- Deliver outbound packs to mailing house

- Outbound stock arrives and correct stock level confirmed
- Print fulfilment packs
- Check samples of fulfilment packs using checklists
- Deliver fulfilment packs to fulfilment house
- Fulfilment stocks arrive and correct stock levels confirmed
- Media buying
- Advertisements appear
- Send mailing tapes/data to mailing house
- Mailing sent
- Response to media advertising/mailing/telemarketing received
- Response information processed to determine fulfilment pack required
- Fulfilment initiated
- Personalised laser letter printing
- Fulfilment packs made up to customer requirements and dispatched
- Fulfilment stocks monitored and replenished if required
- Progress reports received and monitored
- Dispose of unwanted print stocks after campaign close

Telemarketing task list

Telemarketing agency management (applies to external agency or in-house telemarketing team, and inbound and outbound aspects of campaigns)

- Prepare draft telemarketing agency brief using briefing checklist
- Issue draft brief to telemarketing agency (or agencies if competitive tender being used)
- Agency comments on draft brief
- Brief finalised and confirmed
- Agency submits initial recommendation on campaign approach
- Agency selected
- Costs of recommendations evaluated against expected response
- Comment on recommendations, using checklists
- Agency revises recommendations
- Agency develops decision trees
- Decision trees circulated internally and to client for comment
- Agency presents revised decision trees
- Decision trees for testing agreed

- Agency presents draft scripts
- Scripts circulated internally and to client for comment
- Agency presents revised scripts
- Scripts for testing agreed
- Script screen displays designed
- Screens checked
- Brief training and phoneroom management, and receive comments on screens
- Screen displays amended and implemented
- Data entry procedures determined, including return of questionnaire data to customer database
- Data entry procedures implemented
- Test team selected
- Test team trained
- Make test calls
- Check hard copy output
- Trees and scripts revised after testing
- Screens and data entry procedures revised after testing
- Trees and scripts agreed
- Confirm target customers
- Live date

Telemarketing logistics

- Determine customers to be called and provide telephone numbers
- Select main calling team
- Train calling team (products, offer, etc)
- Confirm timing of calling
- Calling begins
- Call results dispatched to system for processing
- Tapes check and follow up
- Progress reports received and monitored

Checklists

These checklists are extensive. However, they are designed to be customised by marketers to their own requirements, and they can be split up to cover different stages of campaign planning, development and implementation. Use them discriminatingly. Decide which questions are helpful, and build a checklist.

Marketing planning checklist

Value of the customer

- Has the life time value of different types of customer in the target market been identified, in revenue and profit terms?
- Has the amount that could be paid to acquire and then keep them been calculated?
- Has this information been used to target campaigns and to evaluate campaign effectiveness?
- Has the company's system been used to estimate and forecast the value of customers in the target market, in the short and the long term?
- Has the relationship between the probability that a customer in the target market will buy a particular product or service and the history of the company's relationship with him or her (eg responses to previous campaigns, past transactions) been calculated?

Positioning

- How do different types of customers in the target market see the company, its products and services?
- Have simple questionnaires been developed to provide data to profile customers on this basis?
- Has there been a clear statement of how we want customers to perceive the company?
- Have campaigns been planned to achieve this perception and measure the achievement?
- If the perception is achieved, will customers be more receptive to communication from the company?
- Has the receptiveness of customers to direct communication been measured?
- Have the implications been identified of company positioning and branding objectives for choice of which product benefits to emphasise in a campaign, what is said about the company, how to handle responses, and the style and tonality of print communications?

- Will visible branding be consistent across all media?
- Is every element of the campaign, from outbound communication to response handling, consistent with corporate image?

Relationship between marketing and promotional planning

- Does the marketing plan consider different promotional options for achieving each marketing strategy?
- Has this investigation included different combinations of the marketing mix elements (sales force, agents, mail etc)?
- Has it taken account of their relative effectiveness?
- Is each campaign the result of a marketing planning process, starting with objectives, proceeding via analysis of the business environment, to strategies and action plans, including implementation and control procedures to ensure that the plan is implemented?
- Will each campaign yield information to improve knowledge of customers?
- Has the importance for promotional purposes of the sought information been tested?
- Has the customer database been used to analyse the business environment, to identify general and specific opportunities for existing products, competitive threats, and gaps where new products may be needed?
- Has a schedule, showing all planned campaigns, been published and communicated to all parties involved in making campaigns work?
- Does it indicate clearly the media and coverage (products, markets) for each campaign? Is there a clear changes/update procedure for this schedule?
- Have overall marketing communications objectives been decided?
- What is the mechanism for ensuring that these objectives are observed in formulating individual campaign objectives?

Campaign planning checklist

Objectives

- Do campaign objectives include awareness of relevant products and services and of general benefits offered, company positioning and image, overall and relative to competition (eg value for money, comprehensive product range, understanding of customer needs, quality of service, reliability), positioning of relevant products?

- Do campaign objectives fit well with the objectives of other campaigns targeted at the same customers?
- Will customers be able to make sense of the range of offers targeted at them?
- Does the campaign play a coherent part in the marketing of the products concerned and in developing a long term relationship with customers?
- Does the campaign use the principle of concentration-domination-repetition or warming-informing (drip-feed)?
- Are campaign targets realistic, given results for similar campaigns, the current market environment and competitive position?
- Will the campaign generate qualified enquiries for promoted products?
- Is it designed to minimise the complexity of enquiry handling?

Targeting

- Is the target market clearly identifiable, on the company's system or lists?
- Have clear criteria been established for identifying target customers?
- Will the campaign reach decision makers and relevant influencers, customers and others who may be involved in the buying decision?
- Will the campaign reach target customers as cost-effectively as possible, and reach as few customers outside the target market as possible?
- Have target customers been chosen partly because of their responsiveness to direct marketing (response level, speed, quality, type of purchase)?
- Have target customers been over- or under-promoted?
- What are the attitudes, motivations and behaviour of customers, and how do these relate to produce usage and responsiveness to promotion?
- What distinguishes heavy from light users and what are the promotional implications of this?

- Have recency, frequency, amount and category data been analysed for key groups of customers, to identify what is happening to the customer base?
- Has this analysis identified opportunity groups for higher usage and threat groups of customers leaving?
- Do criteria for prioritising between campaigns include potential increases in the value of the customer base?
- Has a balance been struck between accuracy and costs of targeting?

Campaign management

- Have campaign details been entered on the company's system, to enable checking for consistency with other campaigns and for opportunities to combine?
- Is the start and end date for all campaigns clear?
- Have clear procedures been laid out for dealing with issues after close date (eg handling of late responses, disposal of old promotional or product stock)?
- Taking all planned campaigns together, will all the suppliers be able to cope with the anticipated workload?
- Have the main potential bottlenecks been identified (eg response handling, fulfilment equipment and labour, data processing capacity)?
- Has each campaign been coded?
- Has the code been communicated to all parties involved?
- Have all the stages of the promotional campaign been identified, timed and agreed with all relevant parties (eg marketing staff, suppliers)?
- Has enough time been left for each stage?
- If the system has a project management module, has it been used to calculate timings?
- Will each party involved in a campaign be evaluated partly according to whether they delivered on time?
- Has a clear process been established for managing each campaign to and through implementation?
- Have all relevant internal and external staff been informed of this process and agreed it?
- Is there a single point of accountability for running the campaign?

- Who is responsible for the whole campaign and each stage of it?
- Where are those responsible based?
- What is the procedure for contacting those responsible?
- If any amendments are made to campaign details, is there a clear sign off procedure and amendment issue procedure?

Data management

- Have the main data flows in each campaign been identified, and clear procedures been set out to handle them?
- Is the format of data to be sent to every party clearly communicated and understood? If tapes or on-line, data formatting, if print-out, report coverage, names and lay-outs?
- Has the destination of each set of data been specified to the sender?
- Have all the codes been checked?
- If data to be sent to any party is to be categorised or split (eg sent on different tapes), has this been communicated to the relevant parties?

Budgeting

- Have standard formats been used for budgeting?
- Has every category of costs been included?
- Has the end-result been specified — sales, contribution, profit, etc?
- Has the final response level required to achieve the target result been calculated, and all the intermediate response ratios?
- Has the outbound contact volume been determined by these calculations?
- Have response rates likely to be achieved by different selection approaches been calculated?
- Have other ways been sought to achieve the same result?

Briefing and supplier management

Briefing

- Has an internal master brief been drawn up, covering:

  (a) problem definition, eg new product launch, economic factors, competitive, market gap opened up

(b) marketing plans and situation — for all marketing mix variables

(c) competition (main products, details of operation, current and anticipated action, strengths and weaknesses, past and anticipated promotional policies, company strengths and weaknesses versus competition)

(d) target customers (age; sex; needs; decision processes; etc)

(e) current and planned promotional activity

(f) prioritised and quantified objectives (strategic, awareness, positioning, branding, market share protection, customer satisfaction, other attitudes, sales, contribution, market development, higher usage frequency, upgrades, profit, etc)

(g) budgets available

(h) any constraints

(i) the product (major benefits, technical specifications and features, price)

(j) the message, proposition and its substantiation, required take-out, differentiation, etc

(k) mood and tone, eg pride, sense of heritage, celebratory (for new product or service), amazement, reassurance, warmth, friendliness, value for money, amusement

(l) call to action (what the company wants the customer to do as a result of the communication — telephone, fill coupon, visit shop, open letter when it arrives)

(m) timing

(n) measurement criteria and methods

(o) testing strategy

(p) mandatories — inclusion of other logos if joint promotion; restrictions.

- Have all internal and external parties been consulted before finalisation of the brief? Is a draft issued, with time available for comment?
- Have all internal and external parties been briefed in detail (direct marketing agency, telemarketing agency, print houses, fulfilment houses, systems staff, marketing and sales staff, other customer-facing staff)?
- Is the circulation list stated on each brief?
- Is the responsibility for briefing clearly understood?

- If briefing is to be face-to-face, has the briefing meeting been scheduled in time and have all required attendees confirmed attendance?

Supplier management

- Have the exact services required from each supplier at each stage of the campaign been specified and agreed?
- Are they covered by contracts?
- Are there clear measures of delivery (content, time, quality), which can be referred back to in case of dispute or bonus award?
- Are all suppliers aware of the services each provides, responsibilities for each campaign, and contact points?
- Are contact reports issued as a result of each meeting, and circulated to all appropriate parties?

Selection and lists

- Is the database up to date on variables used to select customers?
- Has the quality of the data been tested recently enough by other campaigns?
- How did past campaigns using the same variables to select perform?
- If a trial extract is to be run, has time been made available to examine results of the extract (count, plus characteristics of those selected)?
- Has the importance of each variable used to select been tested?
- Are there test cells in the campaign?
- If an external list is to be used, which? What are its characteristics?
- Have these characteristics been communicated to all involved in processing the list?
- Does the profile of the list match that of the company's actual or potential customers?
- If the company is using a new outside list, what selections are possible, at what cost, what is the minimum selection, what addressing formats are available (labels, tape), is it in postal rebate sequence, postcoded, named: if other data is available from it, what is its delivery time?

Campaign details

Timing

- Will customers be contacted when likely to be receptive to the offer?
- Is the campaign cycle well-timed, from repeated making of the offer, through to enquiry handling and fulfilment?
- Is campaign timing co-ordinated with that of other campaigns?
- Does the timing take into account seasonality or other regularity in buying patterns?
- Does the frequency with which the company's best customers will be contacted match their expectations? Has the effect of frequency on response rates been tested?
- If the campaign has two or more-step sales, has the interval between each step been tested?
- For mailings, is timing of the drop critical?
- If so, has the appropriate class of postage been used?
- For multi-media and multi-step campaigns, has the timing of appearance in different media or the next step been mentioned where relevant?

Contact strategies

- Has the amount that can be afforded for each contact been calculated?
- Is the required response from customers at each stage of the contact strategy clear eg ask for more information, buy?
- Has the contact strategy been mapped out, showing clearly the links between each group of respondents and each response step?
- Have the expected numbers for each contact step been calculated?
- Has the information to be collected at each stage of the contact strategy been determined?

Media choice

- Have different media and contact strategies been tested, including combinations of direct mail, inserts, press, catalogues, telephone (inbound and outbound), electronic (telex, fax, E-mail, viewdata, teletext), TV and radio, competitions, events, take-ones, etc?

- Are the chosen media acceptable and credible to customers?
- Is the choice of media right for the message and the role of each message in moving customers towards the sale, the recipients of the message and the strengths, weaknesses, costs and volume capabilities of each medium?
- Does any use of direct mail exploit its strengths and avoid its weaknesses, ie personal and powerful, contains a lot of information, liked and respected as a source of information but sometimes mistrusted, dependence on list quality for hitting targets, not answering customer's individual questions and answers well or at all?
- Is direct mail used in one or other of its three main uses — as a prime medium, support to other media, or support to distribution channels?
- Does any use of inserts exploit their strengths and avoid their weaknesses, ie increase response 3–6 times over page advertising, ability to test many published media cost-effectively, easy response device, communicate more information than press is capable of but low response compared to mail, subject to overlooking and falling out?
- Does any use of press exploit its strengths and avoid its weaknesses, ie many ways to reach target audience, generates awareness as well as response, offers target audience opportunity to identify themselves, inability to personalise, less specific targeting, position/page dependence, dependence on media buying?
- Does use of catalogues exploit their strengths and avoid their weaknesses, ie contain large amounts of information, viewed as credible information source, kept and referred to, static, out of date quickly, expensive, dependent on skill of layout/design?
- Does use of telephone exploit its strengths and avoid its weaknesses, ie immediate, powerful, interactive, able to find decision maker or target accurately, high acceptability if used in existing relationship, able to answer questions or handle objections, flexible, accurate, controllable, testable in small volumes, able to sell up or across product ranges, but limitation on quantity and quality of information conveyed, strength of customer commitment, dependence on good follow-up, absence of visual contact, risk of intrusiveness, contact cost?
- Will telemarketing be used for cold prospecting, follow up of mail responders, screening or qualifying, list building, improving cus-

tomer service, order taking, keeping informed of progress with problems, servicing smaller accounts, reactivating customers?

- If telemarketing is to be used, will too much pressure be avoided? Will it be implemented professionally? Will staff be recruited and trained to maximise potential?
- Does any use of electronic media exploit their strengths but avoid their weaknesses, ie communicate high volume of information, new, high impact, novelty value, instant update, but can be expensive per contact, limited audience, and creative limitation?
- Have the different media been integrated into a coherent campaign, exploiting the strengths of each to maximise effectiveness and coverage?
- Are the media chosen the most cost-effective for the target market? Is this consistent with the evidence of past promotions?

Products

- Have the products to be used in the campaign been clearly stated? Are they coded? Are prices agreed?
- Will the products be available at the time of the campaign?
- Have procedures for getting the product to the customer, through whatever channels are to be used, been laid out and tested?

The offer

- Have different offers been tested to find the best for the target market?
- Are the benefits promoted by the offer based on an in-depth understanding of target customer behaviour and needs?
- Are at least some of the features and benefits in the offer truly exclusive? Is this expressed clearly and in a customer-oriented way?
- Does the offer compare favourably with competitive offers?
- Is the offer clearly described, so customers cannot be in any doubt as to the exact nature of the offer?
- Have the objectives of the offer been identified (eg to get or focus attention, overcome inertia, stimulate interest, give a reason why the customer should respond immediately, make the response more significant by heightening the perceived value of the offer)?
- Have all options for offer definition been explored (bundling products, time limit, give-aways and incentives)?

- Does the offer avoid personal inducements for customers for whom this would be inappropriate?
- Does the offer have greatest perceived value to the customer, but least cost to the company?
- Does the offer take into account available margin for promotional costs?
- Is the offer designed to bring in the right combination of quantity and quality of response?
- Are reasons given why the customer should buy from the company?
- Does the campaign give customers the information they need to determine whether they should respond to it?

Creative

General

- Are all the campaign elements designed to produce action?
- Is the offer packaged to create a favourable first impression?
- Have different creative approaches been tested?
- Does the creative element reinforce company and product branding?
- Is the creative element in character with the product and the market? The target customer?
- Might the form in which the offer is expressed lead customers to believe personal data about them has been misused?
- Has the agency received or developed a creative brief covering the product or service (what it is and does, what is new or special — features, quality, speed, etc, what it competes with or replaces, advantages and benefits), target market (who the natural prospects for it are, who can be persuaded to buy), what can be said (guarantees, value for money, proof, testimonials, topicality, legal and regulatory constraints, taboos, sacred cows)?
- Does the campaign, and every element of it, take customers through the cycle of attention, interest, desire, conviction and action?
- Has a clear picture been built up about target customers — their names, occupations, positions, characters, hopes, likes, dislikes, hates, fears, leisure activities, and above all needs?

- Does the communication involve the customer? Does it solve the customer's problem? Is it personal?
- Does the communication involve both the head and the heart?
- Does the communication avoid seeming too clever and self-satisfied?
- Is the expression of the benefit of the offer unique?
- Is the offer clear at a glance? Is the proposition clear, precise and concise?
- Does one understandable, clear benefit dominate?
- Does the communication establish a clear, memorable reason for buying?
- Does it concentrate on the key to unlock the customer's mind?
- Has research or any empirical evidence established the power of the idea?
- Does the communication start with a unique benefit or offer, and say why it is important to the customer, why he or she cannot do without it, how it will solve his or her problem or supply his or her need?
- Are claims backed with examples?
- Does the communication concentrate on one selling idea?
- Is that selling idea the best one — the best offer that can possibly be made?
- Is every benefit and reason for taking up the offer mentioned somewhere?
- Is the communication true, believable and sincere?
- Will customers feel the company is honest and knows what it is talking about?
- Does the creative element seize the attention, not with gimmicks but with news of benefits or offers?
- Does it carry news or interesting information?
- Will the communication overcome every obstacle?
- Does the communication admit to obvious obstacles?
- Is conviction built in by guarantees, testimonials, research figures, scientific or independent proof, sales figures, examples of experience of other people or other markets?
- Are facts and figures specific?
- Can the creative element be used in a variety of media?
- Can each creative medium be used in several ways (eg magazine inserts, household distribution, parcel enclosures, directories, take-ones, distribution by staff)?

Print copy

- Does the copy attract attention by highlighting benefits, giving news or awakening curiosity?
- Does the copy capture and develop interest, by amplifying the opening attention getter?
- Does the copy engender and enhance desire, by enlarging on benefits, eg by painting word pictures, showing how customers will use and benefit from the offer, or avoid something they do not want?
- Does the copy foster conviction, by using testimonials, test results, statistics, examples and clear, worthwhile guarantees?
- Does the copy ask for and spur to action, repeatedly, with cut off dates, reasons to act, and reminders of benefits at the point of asking?
- Is the copy in a language that is appropriate for the target market and consistent with company and product branding?
- Does copy length match the extent of qualification needed in enquiries?
- Does the copy express true benefits to customers, in terms of customer objectives, rather than enhanced descriptions of features and advantages?
- Does the headline make clear the uniqueness of the offer?
- Is the headline followed by a paragraph enlarging on its promise? Is this followed by an explanation of why the benefit is critical to the prospect?
- Are subheadings used to tell the story on its own?

Copy style

- Are the sentences short?
- Does one paragraph lead clearly on to the next?
- Is long copy broken up by subheadings?
- Are all pictures captioned?
- Is a PS used?
- Is a letter used?
- Have valuable words been used — new, news, now, at last, announcing, introducing, for the first time, breakthrough, a new kind of, first ever, how to, advice on, why, you, surprising, remarkable, save, improved, offer, bargain, opportunity, discount?

- Have carrying devices been used to continue the flow (but that isn't all, there is one more thing, now — here is the best part, here is all you have to do, more important than that, you'll also receive, so that is why, moreover)?
- Have carrying tricks been used (questions at paragraph end, page ending halfway through a paragraph, at a tantalising point)?
- Have all variations been identified?

Illustrations

- Do pictures or graphics demonstrate the yielding of benefits?
- Do they make customers feel they are already getting the benefits?
- Are they easy to take in, without tricky effects?
- Are people shown, to engender interest?
- Do pictures reflect the copy?
- Do they tell a full and logical story?

Print design and management

Letter design

- Does the length of the copy correspond to desired response rate and accuracy of qualification?
- Is it written to the recipient as an individual, as an acquaintance, in both style and content?
- Is it fully personalised, using all customer data which the recipient would expect the company to have and use?
- Has humour been avoided?
- Has it been made easy to read, by indentations, handwriting, underlining, subheadings?
- Does the copy flow logically? Can each paragraph be written as a sentence, and the letter as a paragraph of connected sentences?
- Does it use a postscript?
- Have enclosures been used and tested — testimonial facsimiles, gifts, ways of showing the product in use, samples, enduring information?

Letter management

- What stock is to be used (code number and description)?
- What is anticipated usage?
- What is minimum stock level to be held by fulfilment house?
- Who is supplying the stock?
- When is it arriving at the mailing or fulfilment house?
- What are target and actual supply lead times?
- When is first stock scheduled to arrive?
- When will stock first be used?
- Who is writing the letter and when?
- Which letterhead address will be used?
- Is special paper to be used? If so, what?

  (a) Reverse pre-printed
  (b) special size
  (c) any unusual characteristics — glossy, embossed, etc (possible problems with lasering)
  (d) continuous stationery for line printing.

- Who is signing the letter?
- Is the signature to be digitised? If so, when? Will it be pre-printed?

Pack management

- Will the pack, in all its variations, fit in the chosen envelope (length and width)? Has a dummy been tested for this?
- Are all folds and items machine-enclosable (if required)?
- Does pack design exploit postal price structures?
- Are all the components of the pack clearly identified and coded?
- Have all variations been identified?
- Has the procedure for managing variations been worked out and programmed?
- Who will sign off the pack? Will changes in procedures be notified?
- Who requires samples of the pack?
- What is the procedure for managing variations in the pack components?
- If there is a change, what is to be done with the old stock?

Catalogue

- Is the catalogue designed to be part of a well-established relationship?
- Will it be a permanent salesperson the year round?
- Does it contain information of value in itself?
- Does it sell a full range of products and services without further explanation?
- Have hot spots been identified? Are lead products and services in them?
- Are products sequenced to maximise readership of the whole catalogue?
- Is the catalogue designed to be easy to use and readable?
- Have the right number of order forms been included, in the right places?
- Is the catalogue as widely distributed as it should be?

Order forms

- If detachable from carrying media, will the medium and form still work?
- Does the form ask for the order?
- Is the form reply paid, or is there a first class reply envelope?
- Is the customer's name and address printed on the form?

Envelopes

- Is the envelope overprinted in character with the offer? If so, how?
- Is it machine fillable and standard size? If not, what are its characteristics?
- Does it have a window? Will alignment with the address be correct?
- Could it be perceived as a low quality mailing (or dangerous object)?
- Does the outer envelope have a return address, for undelivered mailings?
- Where is the return address to be printed? Which address?
- What instructions should be given to returner?
- Is it to be sent first or second class?

Response handling and fulfilment

Response method

- Is the desired response clear?
- Are customers told to take action, now, and given the means to do it?
- Are they told why now is important — in benefit terms?
- Do the mode of response and the response vehicle stand out?
- Is the offer restated on the reply card to reinforce and remind at the point of commitment and in case it becomes detached?
- Is a return address given?
- Is a telephone number offered for quick response?
- Is the response vehicle coded?
- If the response vehicle is telephone, does the code and/or the offer to be quoted stand out clearly?
- Has a response handling script (with variations if required) been written and staff trained to use it?
- Is automatic call logging and distribution used?
- Is the mailing package personalised, where possible?
- Is there a direct ordering option, where relevant?
- Is there a reply envelope rather than a card, for where security (money enclosed) or confidentiality (information given) is important?
- Is a reply envelope necessary and/or cost-effective? Should it be a business-reply envelope, stamped, via Freepost?
- Has the physical communication been researched and ideally tested?

Management

- Have all possible responses that customers might make to the campaign been identified, and provision made for handling them?
- Have the resources required for implementing the campaign, including delivering the outbound communication, handling the response and fulfilment, been identified and allocated well in advance?
- Will all staff involved in fulfilment or in handling customers be briefed about the campaign and their role in it?
- Has the team been given time to respond to the brief?
- Have staff been properly trained and motivated?

- Have all actions required to ensure feedback of response and fulfilment data to the database system been taken?
- Will all responses actually arrive at the correct destination quickly and be dealt with quickly?
- If responses are to be prioritised, have the criteria for prioritising been clearly specified and communicated to those implementing it?
- Has the fulfilment house been briefed on likely response volumes?
- Have they been given the media/outbound calling/initial mailing schedule? Will schedule changes be notified to them?
- If responses are being stored on the company's system and accumulated before being sent to the fulfilment house, will they be kept informed of the volume as it accumulates?
- Will all campaign results be clearly identifiable?
- Has every response vehicle been identified as belonging to the campaign?
- Is the manner in which fulfilment is to be carried out consistent with company branding?
- How are returns to be handled?

Telemarketing management

- Are call objectives and decision trees planned and embodied in scripts?
- Is each call planned, under control, monitored and measured?
- Is the data resulting from each call clearly specified and routed?
- Has every campaign element been tested?
- Is the whole campaign properly budgeted, with careful control and measurement of costs and quality?

Monitoring, control and testing

Monitoring and control

- Is every aspect of the campaign being monitored, including the performance of all involved in the fulfilment process (not just amount of fulfilment, but speed and quality)?
- Is a mainstream and exception reporting system in place?
- Are the monitoring and reporting roles of the different parties involved in a campaign clear and agreed?
- Will the sources of all responses and sales be trackable?

- Have all criteria for measuring the campaign been identified (eg reach, leads, sales, profit, attitudes)?
- Has a proper cost-benefit calculation been performed, and will this be computed at the end of the campaign?
- Have you worked out the range of likely responses at each stage of the campaign, to allow the approach to be changed if measures fall outside this range?
- Will all important variables be measured?
- Do variables enable comparison with other media?
- Are different measures used, to aid learning and comparability with other media, eg cost per mailing, per phone call, per lead, per hour, per order, volumes achieved at every stage of contact strategy, ratios between action steps, returns, gone-aways, correspondence received, cross-selling and up-selling?
- Will research be carried out to check the effect of campaigns on attitudes and perceived branding?
- Has an analysis schedule been set up?
- Will the results of analysis be acted upon?

Testing

- Has a control been set up?
- Are key campaign elements tested: targeting, timing, offer, creative?
- Are tests run on large enough samples to be valid?
- Is testing "all or one" or "cross-over"?
- Have likely market-place changes at time of test been taken into account?
- Will roll-out be under same conditions as test (cost, target market, time of year, etc)?

Index

Index

Index

Index

Staffing, of direct marketing management
    campaigns 79
  responsibilities 80–1
Standards, and creativity 42
Statistical analysis 37, 232
Statistician 192
Statuses of campaigns, and authorities 73–9
Strategies, marketing 20–1
Strategy, task list 235
Submitted status 74, 78
Suppliers, use of Form 1 95
  use of Form 6 107
  alternative schemes 171–2
  communication with management
    information systems 215
  contract finalisation 184–6
  costs of 167–73
  management of 66–7, 165–86, 226–7
    checklist 247
    relationship management 4, 173–6
    skill required 199–200
  management abilities of 166–7
  negotiation with 169, 176–84
  relationship management 4, 173–6
  selection 166
  types 165
Systems, management information 211–33
  alternative systems 212–13
  integration with database 213
  needs 212, 214–17
Systems aspect 7, 10–11
Systems feedback reports, Form 19 135–6
Systems specialist 191–2
Systems staff, relationships 4

Target markets 19
  use of Form 5 105
Targeting, in campaigns 5, 36–9
  checklist 243–4
  co-ordination 72
  fine targeted marketing 225
Targeting and scheduling processes 9–10
Task lists 235–40
Telemarketing, integration 35
  skills required 197–8
  task list 239–40
  use of Form 20 137–9
  use of Form 21 140–1
Telemarketing agency management, task list
  239–40
Telemarketing management, checklist 258
Tendering, for suppliers 173–4
Testing, checklist 259
  in direct marketing 5, 48–9
  of lists 48
  planning of 28
  of profiling validity 37
  strategies and priorities, database 224
  use of Form 2 97
Time planning sheets 86
Timing, of campaigns 39–40
  of projects 55–6
Training, in direct marketing 205–9
  of marketers 10, 21
  of sales force 21

Under development status 74, 78

Variance analysis 232